The Magic Word
Complete and Unabridged

©2010 Wilder Publications

All rights reserved. Printed in the United States of America. No part of this book may be used or reproduced in any manner without written permission except for brief quotations for review purposes only.

Wilder Publications, Inc.
PO Box 243
Blacksburg, VA 24060-0243

ISBN 10: 1-61720-002-6
ISBN 13: 978-1-61720-002-1
First Edition

10 9 8 7 6 5 4 3 2 1

The Magic Word
By Robert Collier

Table of Contents

THE MAGIC WORD

The Law of Increase. 5

In the Beginning. 10

Treasure Mapping for Supply. 17

"Wanted: Rain!". 22

Catalysts of Power. 32

The First Commandment. 34

The Three Laws of Life. 48

A Prayer for Work. 57

First Causes. 61

Strong Desire Essential to Success. 76

Magnetic Power of Desire. 80

The Master Formula for Getting What You Want. 85

Putting Power into Your Desire. 95

THE LAW OF INCREASE

I am Success, though hungry, cold, ill-clad,
I wander for a while, I smile and say,
"It is but a time, I shall be glad
Tomorrow, for good fortune comes my way.
God is my Father, He has wealth untold,
His wealth is mine—health, happiness and gold."

—ELLA WHEELER WILCOX

In a pamphlet written by Don Blanding, he tells of a time during the trying years of the Great Depression, , when he found himself financially, mentally and physically "broke." He was suffering from insomnia and from a physical lethargy amounting almost to paralysis. Worst of all, he had a bad case of "self-pity," and he felt that the self-pity was fully justified.

He was staying at a small Art Colony (on credit), trying to rebuild his wrecked life and wretched body. Among those at the Colony was Mike, an Hawaiian boy. Mike seemed to be always cheerful. Mike seemed to be always prosperous. And, naturally, Blanding wondered why. For Mike, when he had known him before, had been blessed with few of this world's goods.

So one day he asked Mike what good fairy had waved her wand over him and turned all that he touched into gold.

For answer, Mike pointed to a string of letters he had pasted over his bed—"L-I-D-G-T-T-F-T-A-T-I-M."

Blanding read them, but could make no sense out of them. "What are they, the 'Open, Sesame' to the Treasure Cave?"

"They have been the 'Open, Sesame' for me," Mike told him, and went on to explain how they had helped him. It seems that Mike, too, had experienced his ups and downs, but in the course of one of his "downs," he had happened upon a teacher who showed him the power of PRAISE and THANKFULNESS.

"There is an inherent law of mind," says Charles Fillmore, "that we INCREASE whatever we PRAISE. The whole of creation responds to praise, and is glad. Animal trainers pet and reward their charges with delicacies for acts of obedience; children glow with joy and gladness when they are praised. Even vegetation grows better for those who love it. We can praise our own ability, and the very brain cells will expand and increase in capacity and intelligence, when we speak words of encouragement and appreciation to them."

God gave you dominion over the earth. Everything is your servant, but remember it is said in the Scriptures that God brought every beast and fowl to Adam, *to see what he would call them.* You are like Adam in this, that you can give to everything and everybody with whom you come in contact the name you like. You can call them good or bad. And whatever you call them, that is what they will be—good servants or evil. You can praise or curse them, and as you do, so will they be to you.

There is one unfailing Law of Increase—*"Whatever is praised and blessed, MULTIPLIES!"* Count your blessings and they increase. If you are in need of supply, start in now to praise every small piece of money that comes to you, blessing it as a symbol of God's abundance and love. Salute the Divinity represented by it. Bless Him and name Him Infinite and Abundant Supply. You will be surprised how soon that small piece of money will increase to many pieces. Take God into your business. Bless your store, bless every one that works for you, each customer that comes in. Know that they represent the Divinity called Abundance, so bless them as such.

If you are working for someone else and want a better job or more pay, start by BLESSING and being THANKFUL *for what you have.* Bless the work you are doing, be thankful for every opportunity it gives you to acquire greater skill or ability or to serve others. Bless the money you earn, no matter how little it may be. Be so thankful to God for it that you can give a small "Thank Offering" from it to someone in greater need than yourself.

Suppose the Boss does seem unappreciative and hard. Bless him just the same. Be thankful for the opportunity to SERVE faithfully, no matter how small the immediate reward may seem to be. Give your best, give it cheerfully, gladly, thankfully, and you will be amazed how quickly the INCREASE will come to you—not necessarily from your immediate boss, but from the Big Boss over all.

I remember reading a letter from a woman in the drought belt in which she said that they, unlike most of their neighbors, had an abundant supply of water, and excellent crops. "When my husband plows a field," she writes, "I ask God to bless each furrow. Each seed that goes into the seeder is blessed, and the realization held that it will produce abundantly according to His righteous law. Our neighbors marveled at the abundance of hay that we cut this year. The hay was sold before the third cutting was put up.

"Each day, in the silence, I put the ranch 'Lovingly in the hands of the Father.' I ask God to bless everybody that comes in contact with the ranch."

Few realize the power of praise and blessing. Praise may be called the great liberator. You remember the story of Paul and Silas. They lay in jail bound with chains, but they did not despair. They rejoiced and sang hymns of praise, and lo, the very walls were shaken down and they were set free.

Praise always magnifies. When we praise God and then look about us and praise His invisible presence in all that we see, we find that the good is so magnified that much becomes evident that we ordinarily fail to see. Running through all of Jesus Christ's acts as well as His teachings we find the glowing element of praise. When He looked at five loaves and two small fishes and realized that He had a multitude to feed, His first thought was a thought of praise. "And looking up to heaven, he blessed."

Go back over the Old Testament and see how often you are adjured to "Praise the Lord and be thankful, that THEN shall the earth yield her increase." Probably no life chronicled in the Scriptures was more beset with trials and dangers than that of King David. And what was his remedy? What brought him through all tribulations to power and riches? Just read the Psalms of David and you will see.

> *Jehovah reigneth; let the earth rejoice;*
> *Let the multitude of isles be glad.*
> *Bless Jehovah, O my soul;*
> *And all that is within me,* bless *his holy name . . .*
> *Who forgiveth all thine iniquities;*
> *Who healeth all they diseases.*

"If anyone could tell you the shortest, surest way to all happiness and all perfection," wrote William Law, "he must tell you to make it a rule to yourself to thank and praise God for everything that happens to you. For it is certain that whatever seeming calamity happens to you, if you thank and praise God for it, you turn it into a blessing. Could you therefore work miracles, you could not do more for yourself than by this thankful spirit; for it turns all that it touches into happiness."

How then can YOU increase your supply? How can you get more of riches and happiness and every good thing of life? In the same way as the Wise Men and the Prophets of old. In the same way that Jesus twice fed the multitudes. In the same way that He filled the disciples' nets to overflowing with fish, after they had labored all night and caught nothing.

By EXPANDING what you have! And the way to expand is through love, through praise and thanksgiving— through saluting the Divinity in it, and naming it Infinite and Abundant Supply.

Throughout the Bible we are told—"In everything by prayer and supplication WITH THANKSGIVING let your requests be made unto God." Again and again the root of inspiration and attainment is stressed. *Rejoice, be glad, praise, give thanks!*

And that was what our Hawaiian boy had done. That was the secret of his prosperity and success. The Talisman he had pasted over his bed meant—"Lord, I do give Thee thanks for the abundance that is mine." Every time he looked upon it, he repeated those words of thankfulness. The happy ending lies in the fact that these words of praise and thanksgiving proved to be as potent a talisman for Don Blanding as they had for Mike, the Hawaiian.

"Whoso offereth praise, glorifieth Me," sang the Psalmist of old. And it is as true today as it was thousands of years ago. Praise, thankfulness, understanding—these three supply the golden key to anything of good you may desire of life.

In "Think What You Want" magazine, some time ago, H. W. Alexander told how praise helps. "Sincere praise is money in your pocket," he said.

It is a spiritual and moral uplift. It is a tonic to the giver and the receiver. It rebounds to both a thousand times. I know a company whose sales during the depression went from $2,600,000 a year to $8,000,000. Praise was the inspiration.

In a divorce court not so long ago was recorded the story of a man who from a laborer's job climbed to the Presidency of his business. A friend asked him why he quit his almost lifetime companion, though she was well provided for. Said he, "Well my wife of today appreciates my ability, tells me right along, wheras my childhood sweetheart knows my weaknesses and tells me about them. I like appreciation." His income tax is on a $100,000 salary.

Little things count. Your secretary has a new dress, a new hat, a fashionably fluffy ruffle—tell her so. The file clerk finds your letters quickly—tell her so. The cop on the beat is sure to see the school boys are safely over with a wave of his hand. Tell him he is tops.

One of the finest persons who worked for me was an elderly servant woman. She had a tough time in life, poorly educated, used split infinitives, came early in the morning to clean the house. She often said to me as I left in the morning, "Sure, you look good today. You've got a big job, you work hard, you'll win." She *thought* I was good, and when I went out I *was* good. Top executives who read this know very well the truth of what the chauffeur, maid, gardener—who gives them a cheery word of praise, means to them at market time, conference time, or directors' time—it rings in their mind— oh, yes, they remember. You can't fly too high.

And the mother who *thinks* her boy or girl is about right, aids them on as no one else can.

I have this belief—that big or little, praise does win friends, wins respect for yourself, wins you a monetary return, and it helps a Pullman porter, a housewife, an industrialist to bigger, better things. It costs you nothing but a smile—but do be sincere.

To the wives who may read this: You know your man. He can't fool you. But be just as honest as you can, praise him, send him out to work with a smile, with praise, and you'll wear sables—try it.

Like attracts like. Praise and appreciation bring back greater praise and appreciation to you. If you want health, happiness, in your life, if you are seeking riches and success, attune your thoughts to these. BLESS the circumstances that surround you. Bless and praise those who come in contact with you. Bless even the difficulties you meet, for by blessing them, you can change them from discordant conditions to favorable ones, you can speed up their rate of activity to where they will bring you good, instead of evil. It is only lack of RESPONSIVENESS to good that produces the lacks in your life. Good works on the plane of EXPANSION. Good revolves at a high rate of activity. You can key your activity to that same rate by an expectant, confident state of mind. You can bring all your surroundings and circumstances up to that same level by BLESSING them, PRAISING the good in them, saluting the DIVINITY in them.

In the pages that follow, we shall show you how the practice of blessing and praising all things has brought good to all who have tried it, how you can use these same methods to attract every good thing *you* may desire.

Into whatsoever house ye enter, first say—"Peace be to this house!"

IN THE BEGINNING

For life is the mirror of king and slave,
'Tis just what we are and do;
Then give to the world the best you have,
And the best will come back to you.

We often speak of psychology and metaphysics as new sciences, and think that the study of these began within the last half-century. Yet if you refer to the very first book of the Bible, you find more profound examples of applied psychology than in any textbook of today.

Take the story of Jacob as an instance. You remember how Jacob agreed to serve Laban seven years for the hand of Rachel in marriage. And how, through the guile of his father-in-law, Jacob had to serve a second seven years. Even then, when he would have gone back to his own country, Laban begged him to tarry yet a while longer, and agreed to pay Jacob as wages "all the speckled and spotted cattle and all the brown cattle among the sheep, and the speckled and spotted among the goats."

Since Laban first removed from the herds all cattle of this kind, the chances of Jacob's getting rich on the speckled offspring of solid-colored cattle seemed poor indeed.

But Jacob evidently knew his Scriptures, and the idea we think so new, that first comes the "word" (or mental image), then the physical manifestation, was in his mind even when he made the bargain.

For what did he do?

And Jacob took him rods of green poplar, and of the hazel and chestnut tree; and pilled white strakes in them, and made the white appear which was in the rods.

And he set the rods which he had pilled before the flocks in the gutters in the watering troughs when the flocks came to drink, that they should conceive when they came to drink.

And the flocks conceived before the rods, and brought forth cattle ringstraked, speckled, and spotted.

And Jacob did separate the lambs, and set the faces of the flocks toward the ringstraked, and all the brown in the flock of Laban; and he put his own flocks by themselves, and put them unto Laban's cattle.

The Magic Word

As it came to pass, whensoever the stronger cattle did conceive, that Jacob laid the rods before the eyes of the cattle in the gutters that they might conceive among the rods.

But when the cattle were feeble, he put them not in; so the feebler were Laban's, and the stronger Jacob's.

And the man increased exceedingly, and had much cattle, and maidservants, and menservants, and camels, and asses.

You have heard of the English cuckoo. Too lazy to rear and care for its own young, it goes to the nests of other birds when they are off seeking food, notes the markings on their eggs, then comes back later *and lays in their nest eggs of those same exact markings!*

Various saints of the middle ages are said to have had markings on their hands, feet and sides similar to those on the crucified Saviour, acquired from constant contemplation of His image. And only recently I read of an adopted child, which was reported to have developed markings similar in all respects to those of the real son of its foster-parents, although the son had died some months before the adopted child was born. The parents were satisfied it was a case of reincarnation, but it seemed to me merely a materialization in the foster-child of the images in the mother's mind. She had grieved inexpressibly over her loss. She had adopted the waif to try to fill the void left by her own little boy. And striving to see in his every action some reminder of her lost one, those images so strongly held in her mind actually expressed themselves in the body of her foster-child.

It all comes back to that first line of the first chapter of the Gospel of St. John—"In the beginning was the Word." For what is a "Word"? A mental image, is it not? Before an architect can build a house, he must have a mental image of what he is to build. Before you can accomplish anything, you must have a clear mental image of what it is you want to do. Turn to the Scriptural account of the creation of the world. What is the outstanding fact you find there?

IN EVERY THING GOD CREATED, THE "WORD CAME FIRST— THEN THE MATERIAL FORM!

Just listen: "And God said, Let there be light... And God said, Let there be a firmament . . . And God said, Let us make man ..."

First the "word," then the material form. Scientists tell us that words denote ideas, mental concepts—that you can always judge how far a race has advanced in the mental scale by the number of words it uses. Its vocabulary is the measure of its ideas. Few words—few ideas, few mental images.

Therefore, when God said—"Let the earth bring forth grass," He had in mind a clear mental image of what grass was like. In other words, He had already formed the mold. As the Scriptures put it—"The Lord God made the earth and the heavens, and every plant of the field *before it was in the earth,* and every herb of the field *before it* grew." He made the mental image, the mold. It needed then only to draw upon the energy about Him to fill that mold and give it material form.

And that is all you, too, need to do to give your word of power material form—first make the mental image, the mold, then pour into it the elements necessary to make that image manifest for all to see.

What do you want first?—Health—Happiness? Riches?

For perfect health, begin by taking the life out of every distorted image of sickness or imperfection. Charge those nerve centers of yours to withdraw their supporting hands, and let your image of disease collapse like the pricked bubble it is.

THEN IMAGE THE PERFECT MOLD OF WHATEVER ORGAN HAS BEEN DISEASED.

Image the perfect mold of it so vividly that you can clearly see it in your mind's eye, then charge The God in You to reach out with its millions of hands for all the elements it needs to make that perfect image manifest.

First the word (the mental image), then the creation. But the creation will never become manifest without faith. So when you have made your image, when you have set The God in You to work pouring into it the elements it needs for life, *"believe that you receive!"* See with the eyes of your mind that perfect organ functioning as it was meant to, *and thank God for it!*

For riches, the same principle holds true. Take your life out of every image of debt, of lack, of unfulfilled obligation. The God in you is a God of plenty. He cannot owe money. He cannot be limited. There are no circumstances powerful enough to force Him to live in poverty or want.

Yet He, remember, is devoted entirely to your advancement. So how can you be tied down by debt or limitation of any kind?

How? Because YOU have insisted upon it. Instead of a God of plenty, you have worshiped one of want. Instead of reaching out for what you needed, you have tied the hands of The God in You and tried to do their work with the paltry powers of your material hands.

Unloose The God in You! Give Him a job and set Him to work. Make your mental image of the great business or other service you long for, then set The God in You to work bringing to you every element you need to make that image real. And don't wait until you receive the whole of it, but as fast as any element becomes manifest, USE it!

If you have only 10-cents, USE it to start your great idea. If you have only the idea, START it, even though you can take only the first step. First the word, remember, then the creation. And there can be no creation without faith.

Show your faith by using each element as fast as it makes itself manifest, even though there be no sign that any other element is following, and before you know it, your whole structure will be complete.

Have you ever read Genevieve Behrend's account of how she got $20,000, when, from all material points of view, her chances of ever seeing that amount of money were just about nil?

"Every night before going to sleep," she writes, in YOUR INVISIBLE POWER:

I made a mental picture of the desired $20,000 which seemed necessary to go and study with Troward. Twenty imaginary $1,000 bills were counted over each night in my bedroom, and then, with the idea of more emphatically impressing my mind with the fact that this twenty thousand dollars was for the purpose of going to England, and studying with Troward, I wrote out my picture, saw myself buying my steamer ticket, walking up and down the ship's deck from New York to London, and finally saw myself accepted as Troward's pupil. This process was repeated every morning and every evening, always impressing more and more fully upon my mind Troward's memorized statement: "My mind is a center of Divine operations." I endeavored to keep this statement in the back part of my consciousness all the time, with no thought in mind of how the money might be obtained. Probably the reason why there was no thought of the avenues through which the money might reach me was because I could not possibly imagine where the $20,000 would come from. So I simply held my thought steady and let the power of attraction find its own way and means.

One day while walking on the street, taking deep breathing exercises, the thought came: "My mind is surely a center of Divine operation. If God fills all space, then God must be in my mind also; if I want this money to study with Troward that I may know the truth of Life, then both the money and the truth must be mine, though I am unable to feel or see the physical manifestations of either. Still," I declared, "it must be mine."

While these reflections were going on in my mind, there seemed to come up from within me the thought: "I AM all the substance there is." Then, from another channel in my brain the answer seemed to come, "Of course, that's it; everything must have its beginning in mind. The Idea must contain within itself the only one and primary substance there is, and this means money as well as everything else." My mind accepted this idea, and immediately all the tension of mind and body was relaxed. There was a feeling of absolute certainty of being in touch with all the power Life has to give. All thought of money, teacher, or even my own personality, vanished in the great wave of joy which swept over my entire being. I walked on and on, with this feeling of joy steadily increasing and expanding until everything about me seemed aglow with resplendent light. Every person I passed appeared illuminated as I was. All consciousness of personality had disappeared, and in its place there came that great and almost overwhelming sense of joy and contentment.

That night when I made my picture of the twenty thousand dollars it was with an entirely changed aspect. On previous occasions, when making my mental picture, I had felt that I was waking up something within myself. This time there was no sensation of effort. I simply counted over the twenty thousand dollars. Then, in a most unexpected manner, from a source of which I had no consciousness at the time, there seemed to open a possible avenue through which the money might reach me. Just as soon as there appeared a circumstance which indicated the direction through which the twenty thousand dollars might come, I not only made a supreme effort to regard the indicated direction calmly as the first sprout of the seed I had sown in the absolute, but left no stone unturned to follow up that direction, thereby fulfilling my part. By so doing, one circumstance seemed naturally to lead to another, until, step by step, my desired twenty thousand dollars was secured.

For happiness, the method is no different. Your God is a God of love, and real love can know no unhappiness, for love gets its happiness from giving.

There are laws to interfere with almost every other activity of humanity, but none to keep you from giving as much as you like. An unselfish giving results in getting, just as surely as planting results in harvesting. Give with no thought of reward but the good of the one you are helping, and good is bound to flow back to you.

Love begets love, you know, so take your life out of every thought of enmity, of repining, of unhappiness. In place of these, see yourself in your mind's eye giving every manner of happiness to all whom you would have love you. Image that in your mind's eye, then set The God in You to work bringing you opportunities to make all these loved ones happier. And as fast as each opportunity presents itself, USE it! No matter how tiny an opportunity it may be, *use it!* No matter if it be merely the chance to say a pleasant word, to give a kindly smile, to bring a happy thought, *use it!*

And in the using, you will find that doubly great happiness has come to you.

Each of us is a miniature sun, his circumstances and surroundings his solar system. If debts and disease and troubles form part of your system, what is the remedy? *Let go of them, of course!* If you want new planets of riches and youth and happiness, how can you get them? In the same way the sun does, and only in that way—by throwing off from yourself.

Remember this: Nothing can come into your solar system except from you or through you. If it comes from outside, it is not yours and has no power over you until you take hold of it mentally and accept it as yours. If you don't want it, you can refuse to accept it, refuse to take hold of it, refuse to believe in its reality—then put in the place it seems to occupy, the perfect condition of your own imaging.

If there is something lacking in your solar system, you have only to "speak the word"—create the mental image, then hold to that image in serene faith until The God in You has filled it with those elements that make it visible to all.

It is your own fault when you allow yourself to become the victim of personal impotence or of undesirable external situations. As Emerson put it—"Nothing external to you has any power over you." You fear these negative seemings simply because you BELIEVE in them, when all the time it is only that BELIEF that gives them power and authority.

Remember, YOU are the central sun of your own solar system. YOU have dominion over everything within that system. YOU can say what shall enter, what shall stay there. And you have infinite attractive power to draw to you anything of good you may desire. Nothing stands between you and your fondest desires but lack of understanding of or faith in this power of attraction.

But once you send out the desire, you must have perfect faith in the result. You cannot accomplish anything by expressing a desire and then spending your time fearing and worrying lest you will not find the work you seek, or not have the money in time to pay your bills, or that some other evil thing will happen to prevent good from coming to you. The law of attraction cannot bring both good and evil at the same time. It must be one or the other. And it is up to YOU to decide which it shall be.

"After any object or purpose is clearly held in thought," says Lilian Whiting, "its precipitation in tangible and visible form is merely a question of time.

Columbus saw in vision a path through trackless waters around the world. The vision always precedes and itself determines the realization."

Dare you to say—"Every day in every way I am getting richer and richer"? If you dare—and will follow up the word with the mental image of yourself HAVING all the riches you desire—Spirit substance will make your word manifest and show you the way to riches.

You were designed by the Father to be master of your fate and captain of your soul. If you are not exercising that mastery, it is because you are lying down on the job. Instead of mastering your thoughts and mental images, you are letting them bow down before mere things.

No thing can make you unhappy if you "will exercise your divine power of love and blessings towards it. Everything is good in its essence, and that good essence will respond to your call of blessing, and its good will come forth to meet you.

> *The world stands out on either side*
> *No wider than the heart is wide;*
> *Above the world is stretched the sky—*
> *No higher than the soul is high;*
> *The heart can push the sea and land*
> *Farther away on either hand;*
> *The soul can split the sky in two,*
> *And let the Face of God shine through.*

TREASURE MAPPING FOR SUPPLY

So many people have won to success and happiness by making "Treasure Maps" to more easily visualize the things they wanted, that "Nautilus" magazine recently ran a prize competition for the best article showing how a "Treasure Map" had helped to bring about one's heart's desire. Caroline J. Drake won the contest.

"I had been bookkeeper," she wrote, "in a large department store for seven years when the manager's niece, whose husband had just died, was put in my place.

I felt stunned. My husband had died ten years previously, leaving a little home and some insurance. But sickness and hospital bills had long since taken both home and money. I had supported the family for eight years and kept the three children in school, but had not been able to save any money. The eldest child, a boy, had just finished high school but as yet had found nothing to do to help along.

Day after day I looked for work of any kind to do which might pay rent and give us a living. I was thirty-five years old, strong, capable and willing; but there was absolutely no place for me. For the first time in my life I was afraid of the future. The thought that we might have to go on relief appalled me.

Thus three months passed. I was behind two months with the rent when the landlord told me I would have to move. I asked him to give me a few days longer in which to try and find work. This he agreed to do.

The next morning I started out again on my rounds. In passing a magazine stand I stopped and glanced over the papers and magazines. It must have been the answer to my many prayers that led me to pick up the copy of a magazine which stared me in the face. Idly I opened it and glanced at the table of contents. My mind was in such a turmoil that I was barely conscious of the words which my eyes saw.

Suddenly my eye was caught by a title about 'treasure-mapping' for success and supply. Something impelled me to buy a copy of the magazine, which proved to be the turning point in our lives.

Instead of looking for work, I went home. Still under the influence of that "Something" (which I did not then understand) I began to read the magazine. Strange and unreal as it then seemed, still I did not doubt. I read each article eagerly and in its order. When I came to the article about treasure-mapping to bring success and supply, something about the idea seemed to hold me in its grip. As a child I had always loved games, and this idea of making a treasure-map reawakened that old desire.

I read the article several times. Then, with a bunch of papers which I hunted up, I set to work to make my treasure-map of success and supply. So many things came into my mind to put on that treasure-map! First, there was the little cottage at the edge of town. Then there was a little dress and millinery shop which I had always longed for. Then, of course, a car. And in that cottage would be a piano for the girls; a yard in the back where we could work among the flowers of an evening or a morning. My enthusiasm grew by leaps and bounds. From magazines and papers I cut pictures and words and sentences—all connected with the idea of success and abundance.

HOW I MADE THE "TREASURE-MAP"

Next I found a large sheet of heavy white paper and began building that map. In the center I pasted a picture of a lovely little cottage with wide porches and trees and shrubbery around it. In one corner of the map I put a picture of a little storeroom and underneath I pasted the words, "Betty's Style Shop." Close to this I pasted pictures of a few very stylish dresses and hats.

At different places on the map I placed sentiments and mottoes—all carrying out the idea of success, abundance, happiness and harmony.

I do not know how long I worked on that treasure-map which was to be the means of attracting into our lives the things which we had need of and desired. I could already feel myself living in that cottage and working in the little dress shop. Never had I felt so completely fascinated and thrilled with an idea as with that treasure-map and what I was sure it would bring us. I tacked the map on the wall of my bedroom, right in front of my bed, so that the first thing I saw in the morning and the last thing at night would be that treasure-map of my desires.

Every night and morning I would go over every detail of that map until it fairly seemed to become a part of my very being. It became so clear that I could call it instantly to mind at any moment in the day. Then in my Silence period I would see myself and the children going through the rooms of the cottage, laughing and talking, arranging the furniture and curtains. I would picture my daughters at the piano singing and playing; I would see my son sitting in the library with books and papers all around him. Then I would picture myself walking about my shop, proud and happy; people coming in and going out. I would see them buying the lovely hats and dresses, paying me for them and going out smiling.

During all this time, I was learning more and more of the power of the mind to draw to us the things and conditions like unto our thoughts. I understood that this treasure-map was but the means of impressing upon my subconscious mind the pattern from which to build the conditions of success and harmony into our lives. Always, after each of my Silence periods, I would lovingly thank God that the abundance and harmony and love were already ours. I believed that I *had* received; for mentally living in the cottage and working in the shop was to me the certain fact that I would take possession of them in the material world just as in the mental.

When the children found out what I was doing, they entered heartily into the spirit of the game and each of them soon had a treasure-map of his own.

It was not many weeks before things began to happen. One day I met an old friend of my husband's and he told me that he and his wife were going west for several months and asked if we would come out and take care of their house for the rent. A week later we were settled in that cottage, which was almost the very picture of the one I had on my treasure-map. A little later my son was offered work evenings and Saturdays in an engineering office, which proved the means of his entering college that fall.

We had been in the cottage nearly two months when I saw an advertisement in the local paper for a woman to take charge of a lady's dress shop. I answered the ad and found that the owner was having to give up the shop for several months, perhaps permanently, on account of her health. Arrangements were quickly made so that I was to run the business and share half the expenses and the profits.

Within six months after we started treasure-mapping for supply, we had accomplished practically everything that map called for. When the owner of the cottage came back several months later, he made it possible for us to buy the place and we are still here.

The business, too, is mine now. The lady decided not to come back, so I bought the business, paying her so much a month. It is a much larger and more thriving business now—thanks to the understanding of the power of thought which I gained through my study and practice.

In another article in "Nautilus," Helen M. Kitchel told how she used a "Treasure Map" to sell her property. She pasted an attractive picture of her house on a large sheet of paper, put a description of it underneath and then surrounded picture and description with such mottoes as— "Love, the Divine Magnet, attracts all that is good"—and others of a similar nature. She hung her map where she could see and study it several times a day, and repeated some of the affirmations or mottoes whenever the thought of making a sale occurred to her.

She also started a little private letter box which she called "God's Box" and in it, whenever the thought occurred to her, she placed a letter written to God telling of her needs and desires. Then each month she went over the letters, taking out and giving thanks for those that had been answered.

Within a year her house was sold, on the very plan she herself had outlined in one of her "Letters to God," on the exact basis and for the exact price she had asked in that letter.

Another method is to "Talk with God." Go somewhere where you can be alone and undisturbed for a little while, and talk aloud to God exactly as you would to a loving and understanding Father. Tell Him your needs. Tell Him your ambitions and desires. Describe in detail just what you want. Then thank Him just as you would an earthly father with whom you had had a similar talk and "who had promised you the things you asked for. You will be amazed at the result of such sincere talks.

"My word shall not come back to me void, but shall accomplish that whereunto it was sent." Whatever you can visualize—and BELIEVE in—you can accomplish. Whatever you can see as yours in your mind's eye, you can get. "In the beginning was the Word." In the beginning is the mental image.

Corinne Updegraff Wells had an article in her little magazine "Through Rose Colored Glasses" that illustrates the power of visualizing your ambitions and desires. "Many years ago," she says, "a young girl who lived in a New York tenement was employed by a fashionable Fifth Avenue modiste to run errands, match samples and pull basting threads.

Annie loved her job. From an environment of poverty she had become suddenly and miraculously an inhabitant of an amazing new world of beauty, wealth and fashion. It was thrilling to see lovely ladies arrive in fine carriages, to watch the social elite preen before Madam's big gold framed mirrors.

The little errand girl, in her starched gingham, soon became filled with desire and fired with ambition. She began imagining herself as head of the establishment instead of its most lowly employee. Whenever she passed before mirrors she smiled at a secret reflection she saw of herself, older and more beautiful, a person of charm and importance.

Of course, nobody even suspected the secret existence of this make-believe person. Hugging her precious secret, Annie smiled confidently at that dazzling reflection in the mirror and began playing an exciting game, "I'll pretend I'm already Madam. I'll be polite and look my best and have grand manners and learn something new each day. I'll work as hard and take as much interest as though the shop were really and truly mine."

Soon fashionable ladies began whispering to Madam: "Annie's the smartest girl you've ever had!" Madam herself began to smile and say: "Annie, you may fold Mrs. Vandergilt's gown if you'll be very careful," or, "I'm going to let you deliver this wedding dress," or, "My dear, you're developing a real gift for color and line," and, finally, "I'm promoting you to the work-room."

The years passed quickly. Each day Annie came more and more to resemble the image she alone had seen of herself. Gradually the little errand girl became Annette, an individual; then Annette, stylist; and finally, Madam Annette, renowned costume designer for a rich and famous clientele.

The images we hold steadfastly in our minds over the years are not illusions; they are the patterns by which we are able to mould our own destinies.

> *You never can tell when you do an act*
> *Just what the result will be,*
> *But with every deed you are sowing a seed,*
> *Though the harvest you man not see.*
> *Each kindly act is an acorn dropped*
> *In God's productive soil;*
> *You may not know, but the tree shall grow*
> *With shelter for those who toil.*
>
> *You never can tell what your thought will do*
> *In bringing you hate or love,*
> *For thoughts are things and their airy wings*
> *Are swifter than carrier doves.*
> *They follow the law of the universe—*
> *Each thing must create its kind,*
> *And the speed o'er the track to bring you back*
> *Whatever went out from your mind.*

—ELLA WHEELER WILCOX

"WANTED: RAIN!"

From one to two inches, and free from hail if possible. Is badly needed to save remaining crops and fill the reservoirs. Must be delivered soon to do any good. Will pay highest market price.

Can be delivered any place; prefer general rain. Showers gratefully accepted, but prefer real, honest-to-goodness downpour.

This offer made by the following firms for the general good of the community, and in the general belief that anything worth having, is worth asking for.

BELLE FOURCHE, South Dakota needed one thing— RAIN—to save remaining crops and fill the reservoirs. Why not advertise for it, thought L. A. Gleyre, publisher of THE NORTHWEST POST. A novel idea—advertising to the Lord—never been tried in just that way before, but at least there was no harm in trying. The prayerful advertisement reprinted above was the result.

"We proposed to each merchant in town," says Mr. Gleyre, "that he pay $2.50 for his name at the bottom of the page ad, with the provision that if no material rain fell between the date of the advertisement and the following Tuesday midnight, the ad was entirely at our expense.

The idea took immediately . . . we could probably have filled a double truck. While the week was rolling by, our people had a new one to think about—their minds were actually taken off the scarcity of rain and made to function along the line of whether THE NORTHWEST POST was going to make good with their ad. The majority of our merchants were pleased with the idea. Some actually believed we had some inside information from the weather bureau which prompted our offer. A few, including one or two preachers, while not saying so to us, took occasion to say it was sacrilegious, etc.

During the specified week, light rains fell in some parts of our territory. Belle Fourche had three very light sprinkles—not enough to count, for we agreed that the rain should be a downpour. Toward the end of the week excitement ran rife and interest continued to grow. Some of our warm friends made bets we would win. Others openly hoped we would, while everyone agreed that it would be tremendously helpful if we did win.

We *won*—but lost. Just six hours after midnight, Wednesday morning, it rained pitch-forks-and-saw-logs-for-handles. It was exactly what we advertised for—a swash-buckling, rip-snortin' downpour of rain. It measured from one-half to two inches, and one remote point reported seven inches of rainfall!

But we didn't charge any merchant a cent. We lost by six hours.

I think it attracted more attention than anything we have done in years. To this day we are asked to advertise for something needed.

Where did that rain come from? Did the advertisement bring it? Does the Rain Dance of the Hopi Indians bring it? Did the prayer of Elijah bring it, as told in the Bible?

Yes! At least, so we believe, and we think we can show you good reason for that belief. Not only that, but we believe that back of these answers to prayer is the fundamental law of life and supply!

For of all the promises of Jesus, there is but one that promises us WHATEVER WE ASK shall be done for us! That one positive assurance is *based on this condition*—"If two of you agree on earth as touching anything they shall ask, it shall be done for them of my Father which is in Heaven."

And again He said—"Where two or three are gathered together in My name, there am I in the midst of them." Why is this? Why the necessity for several to unite in asking for a thing in order to be sure of getting it?

A good many years ago, Professor Henry of Princeton made an experiment with a charged magnet. First he took an ordinary magnet of large size, suspended it from a rafter and with it lifted a few pounds of iron.

Then he wrapped the magnet with wire and charged it with the current from a small battery. Instead of only a few pounds, the now highly charged magnet lifted 3,000 pounds!

That is what happens when one person prays, believing, and another adds his prayers and his faith. In effect, the second person is charging the magnet of the first one with his current, MULTIPLYING the power of the other's prayer a dozen times over.

In "Nautilus" magazine some months ago, Elizabeth Gregg told how five people prayed—agreeing—and the most pressing personal problem of each was soon solved. It seems that the husband of a Mrs. A. had been sick with ulcerated stomach for months. She had prayed repeatedly, without result, so one day she picked four of her friends whom she knew to be badly in need of help in different ways, and got them to agree to meet together on a certain day each week and see if, by uniting their prayers in perfect agreement, they might not improve their condition.

At the first meeting, it was decided to pray for the recovery of Mrs. A.'s husband, so these five women, sitting in silence, mentally pictured the husband strong and well, going about his work in a happy way. Then they gave thanks that their prayer had been answered.

"It was agreed," the article goes on to say, "that promptly at twelve o'clock noon each day until the next meeting, each of the five women would stop whatever she was doing and spend five minutes in silent prayer, agreeing with each other, that the husband be freed from sickness.

Three days after that first meeting, the husband was entirely free from pain. By the end of the week, he was on his way to complete recovery.

Next came the problem of Mrs. B., a widow whose home was to be sold in six weeks for failure to meet her payments. With earnestness and faith the women concentrated at the stated time each day upon the desire that the way would open for her supply. And true to the law, the way did open. Just a day before the week was up a well-to-do lady in the town called and asked Mrs. B. if she would take care of her children, eight and ten, for a few weeks while she, the mother, was away. The sum she offered would take care of the back payments on the home and provide living expenses. Shortly after the lady returned she made arrangements for Mrs. B. to take care of an invalid aunt, which gave the widow a steady and lucrative income.

Next was the problem of Mrs. C, whose husband had been out of work for several months. A few days after the week of agreement was up the husband received a letter from a cousin living at a short distance offering him work in his lumber mill. So, again the law was fulfilled.

Then the case of little Miss D., who for years had been estranged from her family, came under the law for solution. But in this case it was several weeks before any outward sign of fulfillment appeared. However, love had entered the heart of Miss D. during this time and for the first time since the estrangement she gave way to her new feeling and wrote to each of the family asking forgiveness for what she now acknowledged had been intolerance on her part. By return mail came letters from her family, letters also filled with the spirit of love. Thus, for the fourth time in the work of these women did the law work unfailingly.

The last problem was that of Mrs. E., who owned a little dress shop but whose business had been almost ruined since the larger and newer shop just across the street had opened. Envy and hate had filled the heart of Mrs. E. so that she resisted all overtures at friendship which the owner of the new shop had made. Then, from her study of Truth she learned that no one need compete with anyone; that there is full abundance for all when we learn how to claim it. So, instead of envying, she now joined with the others in sending out love and good will to her competitor, as she had called her.

A few weeks later the owner of the new store called and asked if Mrs. E. would take over the management of her store for six months while she was in the East on business. She explained that when she returned it might be advantageous to both of them to form a partnership. This was later done and today Mrs. E. is half owner of a thriving dress and millinery shop and there is perfect harmony between her and the woman she once hated.

Russell Conwell, author of "Acres of Diamonds," tells of dozens of such cases. He tells of a kidnaped child returned unharmed through the power of united prayer; of a lost child found in the same way; of men and women cured of apparently incurable diseases; of businesses saved, of positions won, of love renewed and families reunited. There is no good thing you can ask, believing, that shall not be given you.

"What will you have?" quoth God. "Pay for it and take it." And the paying consists of complying with the law of agreement, by praying—if you pray alone—that the good you are asking for yourself shall be given to all others as well, by "agreeing as to what ye shall ask" if you are praying in a group.

Did you ever read the diary of George Mueller covering the early days of his great work? George Mueller, you know, was the man who started an orphanage with no money in hand, no rich patrons, no prospects—just absolute trust in God. Read the following extracts from his diary and see how that trust was justified:

Nov. 18, 1830. Our money was reduced to about eight shillings. When I was praying with my wife in the morning, the Lord brought to my mind the state of our purse, and I was led to ask Him for some money. About four hours after, a sister said to me, "Do you want any money?" "I told the brethren," said I, "dear sister, when I gave up my salary, that I would for the future tell the Lord only about my wants." She replied, "But He has told me to give you some money." My heart rejoiced, seeing the Lord's faithfulness, but I thought it better not to tell her about our circumstances, lest she should be influenced to give accordingly; and I also was assured that, if it were of the Lord, she could not but give, I therefore turned the conversation to other subjects, but when I left she gave me two guineas.

On March 7. I was again tempted to disbelieve the faithfulness of the Lord, and though I was not miserable, still, I was not so fully resting upon the Lord that I could triumph with joy. It was but one hour after, when the Lord gave me another proof of His faithful love. A Christian lady brought five sovereigns for us.

April 16. This morning I found that our money was reduced to three shillings; and I said to myself, I must now go and ask the Lord earnestly for fresh supplies. But before I had prayed, there was sent from Exeter two pounds, as a proof that the Lord hears before we call.

October 2. Tuesday evening. The Lord's holy name be praised! He hath dealt most bountifully with us during the last three days! The day before yesterday five pounds came in for the orphans. O how kind is the Lord! Always before there has been actual want he has sent help. Yesterday came in one pound ten shillings more. Thus the expenses of yesterday for housekeeping were defrayed. The Lord helped me also to pay yesterday the nineteen pounds ten shillings for the rent.

I saw more clearly than ever that the first great and primary business to which I ought to attend every day was to have my soul happy in the Lord. The first thing to be concerned about was not how much I might serve the Lord, how I might glorify the Lord; but how I might get my soul into a happy state, and how my inner man might be nourished.

REVIEW OF THE YEAR 1838

As to my temporal supplies. The Lord has been pleased to give me during the past year 350 pounds, 4 shillings, 8 pence. During no period of my life has the Lord so richly supplied me. Truly, it must be manifest that, even for this life, it is by far the best thing to seek to act according to the mind of the Lord as to temporal things. We have to make known our need to God in prayer, ask His help, and then we have to believe He will give us what we need. Prayer alone is not enough. We may pray never so much, yet, if we do not *believe* that God will give us what we need, we have no reason to expect that we shall receive what we have asked for.

"In the heart of man a cry, in the heart of God supply." But as Mueller said, prayer alone is not enough. If we do not BELIEVE that God will give us what we ask for, we have no reason to expect that we shall receive it.

How can we cultivate such belief? Jesus gave us the cue. "Unless ye be converted (turned about) and become as a little child, ye shall in no wise enter the Kingdom of Heaven." And again—"Unless a man be born again, he shall not enter the Kingdom."

How can we become as a little child? How can we be born again? The first essential would seem to be to determine what there is about a child that we must imitate. What one thing is universal with all little children? DE-PENDENCE, is it not? Utter dependence upon those around them, utter faith in them to provide their needs. And the greater the Dependence, the better those needs seem to be supplied.

Take the embryonic child in its mother's womb, for instance. At inception, it measures only .004 centimeters. In nine months, it multiplies in size a billion times. That is what happens to it during its state of most utter dependence. In the next eighteen to twenty-one years, when it comes to depend more and more upon itself, it increases only sixteen times.

The Magic Word

Does that mean we should make no effort ourselves? By no means! The admonition given us was—"Work and pray!" And the "work" is emphasized first. But it does mean that when we have done all that is in our power, we can confidently and serenely leave to the Lord whatever else is necessary to the accomplishment of our desire.

Three thousand years ago, there was a poor woman whose husband had just died and left her with two small sons and a heavy burden of debt.

The amount was not much, as debts go today, but when you have not a cent, even a small debt looks big as a mountain. And the widow had nothing at all.

So in the fashion of those days, her creditor purposed to sell her sons into bondage. For even in those semi-barbaric times, property was more valuable than life. The right of human beings to life, liberty and the pursuit of happiness had never even been heard of. So she, having nowhere else to turn, went to the Prophet Elisha, and begged him to help her in her need.

And what do you suppose Elisha did? Took up a collection? Or appealed to the fund for widows and orphans? Not he! "What have you in the house?" he asked.

He believed in using the means at hand, believing that God always provides unlimited supply if we but have the courage and faith to use what we have.

So he merely asked what the widow had to start with, and when told—"Naught save a pot of oil," he bade her borrow vessels from the neighbors *and pour out into them the oil that she had*. In other words, she was to *start the flow*. And it is written that so long as she had vessels to receive it, *the oil kept flowing*.

When the vessels were all filled, Elisha bade her sell the oil and pay her debt, and then start afresh with her sons beside her.

What have YOU *in your house?* When troubles assail you, do you sit back and bemoan your fate, waiting for some friend to help, or do you take stock of what you have, and set to work using it?

You remember the story of the man who came from the hospital after an accident, completely paralyzed. Of all his body, he could move only one finger. In those circumstances, wouldn't you have given up? But he didn't. "If I can move but one finger," he decided, "I'll use it to do more than one finger ever accomplished before!" He did—and lo and behold! In a little while, the fingers next that one began to show life, too. Before many months had passed, he was using every muscle in his body.

I know of a man who lost everything he had in the clothing business. From an expensive apartment, he had to move his family into the poorest rooms in town, where they and their neighbors did not know from one day to another, where the next meal was coming from. They were downcast—yes. But discouraged? No!

He went around to some of his old creditors—got them to trust him for a few knit neckties that they could not sell anywhere else—found a printer who would give him credit for a few hundred envelopes, letterheads and postage—and sent those ties to lists of men culled from the occupational directory of the telephone book. As fast as the money for them came back, he bought more ties and mailed them out, he and his family doing the work of enclosing, addressing and stamping in their cramped little apartment. Before that type of selling became passe, *he had made two hundred thousand dollars out of it.* Yet most men in the same circumstances give up and quit. Life's biggest mistakes, according to Harrington Emerson, is to under-estimate your power to develop and to accomplish. Ella Wheeler Wilcox says:

> *Ships sail east, and ships sail west,*
> *By the very same breezes that blow;*
> *It's the set of the sails, and not the gales,*
> *That determine where they go.*

Success is not a thing—not a guerdon that awaits you at some far-off shrine. Success lies in doing well whatever thing you are doing *now.* It is more a matter of mental attitude than of mental or physical capacity. You have all the fundamentals of it right now. But it is only the USE of them that can make you successful.

"All very well," perhaps you say, "but look at the handicaps I am under. There is Jim Jones, whose father left him a million—and all mine left was some debts to add to my own."

Have you ever read Emerson's comparison of Alaska and Switzerland? Alaska, according to him, is in six respects much better off than Switzerland. It has tremendous resources of virgin forests; Switzerland has practically none. It has great stores of gold and silver and copper and lead and tin and coal; Switzerland has practically none. It has fisheries—the greatest in the world; Switzerland has none.

It has in proportion to its area, greater agricultural possibilities than Switzerland—over a hundred thousand square miles suitable for agriculture. It has a tremendous seacoast; Switzerland none. And yet if Alaska were supporting the same number of people to the square mile as Switzerland, it would have 120,000,000 inhabitants.

Now the Swiss have marketed what? Natural resources? No! The Swiss are a people who take a block of wood that was worth ten cents and convert it into a carving worth a hundred dollars.

They will take a ton of metal, steel, brass and so on, and put it together in such form as to make it worth several million dollars.

They take cotton thread that they buy from this country at twenty cents a pound, and they convert it into lace worth a couple of thousand dollars a pound.

And because as a nation they have learned the art of utilizing their latent capacities, they have prospered abundantly.

What is the moral? Simply this: It is not money that counts. It is not natural resources. It is the way *you use what you have!* You can succeed with what you have at this moment, if only you learn to use it rightly.

"Ask not for some power that has been denied you. Ask what ability you have which can be made to develop into something worth while. *What is in your hand?*"

"We are too apt to think," says Bruce Barton, "that if we had some other man's equipment or opportunity, we could do great things. Most successful men have not achieved their distinction by having some new talent or opportunity presented to them. They have developed the opportunity that was at hand."

Great successes are simply a group of little successes built one upon another, in much the same way that John MacDonald's first great subway was merely a long line of little cellars—*strung together!* As Professor James put it—

As we become permanent drunkards by so many separate drinks, so we become saints in the moral, and authorities and experts in the practical and scientific spheres, by so many separate acts and hours of working. Let no one have any anxiety about the upshot of his work or education, whatever the line of it may be. If he keeps faithfully busy each hour of the working day, he may safely leave the final result to itself. He can with perfect certainty count on waking some fine morning, to find himself one of the competent ones of his generation, in whatever pursuit he may have singled out.

What makes a great musician? Practice—keeping everlastingly at it until playing becomes second nature. What makes a great artist, a great lawyer, a great engineer, a great mechanic or carpenter? Persevering study and practice. You may have a natural liking for a subject, so the study of it is easier to you than to others, but the big successes in life have seldom been the brilliant men, the natural wonders, the "born orators" or the talented artists. The great successes have been the "grinds."

"A few years ago," said Dr. John M. Thomas, president of Rutgers University, "Rutgers had a student called a 'greasy grind' by some of his classmates. This was S. Parker Gilbert, Agent-General for Reparations under the Dawes plan. He may have been a 'greasy grind,' but at thirty-two he was earning $45,000 a year. And, according to Owen D. Young, Chairman of the Board of Directors of the General Electric Company, Gilbert held for several years the most important political position in the world."

A good many men in and out of college have an idea that to study is foolish. "No one ever gets anywhere from studying," they say. S. Parker Gilbert is only one of thousands of cases that prove to the contrary.

The most important job in the world for you is the one above yours. And the way to get it is to study—to "grind"— until you can put more of knowledge, more of skill, more of initiative into it than any man around you. Only thus can you win success.

Why do so many fail? Because they do not try hard enough, work persistently enough. The doors of opportunity are always closed. They have been since the world began. History tells us of no time when you could walk down a street and find any doors of opportunity standing open and inviting you to come in. Doors that are worth entering are usually closed, but the resolute and courageous knock at those doors, and keep knocking persistently until they are opened.

You remember the parable of the importunate friend:

And He said unto them, Which of you shall have a friend, and shall go unto him at midnight and say unto him, Friend, lend me three loaves; for a friend of mine in his journey is come to me, and I have nothing to set before him?

And he from within shall answer and say, Trouble me not; the door is now shut, and my children are with me in bed; I cannot rise and give thee.

I say unto you, though he will not rise and give him because he is his friend, yet because of his importunity he will rise and give him as many as he needeth. And I say unto you, Ask, and it shall be given you; seek, and ye shall find; knock and it shall be opened to you.

Why do so many fail to receive that for which they ask? Because they are not importunate enough. They do not convince the God in them that their prayer is something they MUST have. They ask and knock once or twice, and because the door is not immediately opened, they give up in despair. Remember—"He that wavereth is like a wave of the sea, driven with the wind and tossed. Let not that man think that he shall receive anything of the Lord."

If you have faith in God or man or self,

The Magic Word

Say so; if not, push back upon the shelf
Of silence all your thoughts till faith shall come.
No one will grieve because your lips are dumb.
— ELLA WHEELER WILCOX

CATALYSTS OF POWER

Doubt not, fear not, work on, and wait;
As sure as dawn shall conquer dark,
So love will triumph over hate,
And Spring will bring again the lark.
—DOUGLAS MALLOCH

Nearly two thousand years before Christ, it was said in the Vedas (the sacred writings of the Hindoos) that if any two people would unite their psychic forces, they could conquer the world, even though singly they could do nothing.

Then came Jesus to tell us even more positively that if two of us agree as touching anything we may ask, it shall be done for us.

Jesus never made any such positive promise of certain results when we pray alone. Why should it be necessary for two to unite their desires or prayers in order to be sure of results? If you add 2 to 2, you get only 4. If you add your muscular power to mine, you can lift only twice as much as either of us could lift alone. Yet if you add your prayers to mine, you get—not merely twice the power, but a hundred or a thousand times as much.

Why should this be? We have the word of many great psychologists that it is so. Judge Troward of England, who was to the British Empire what Professor Wm. James was to America, is authority for the statement, as is Brown Landone and a score of psychologists of lesser note. What is the reason?

Perhaps the answer lies in what the chemists call CATALYSTS. In chemistry there are certain substances which, when added to others, release many thousands of times as much power as they themselves contain. These catalysts, without losing any of their own energy, multiply the energy in other substances by thousands and sometimes even by millions! Perhaps that is what happens when two or more unite as touching the thing they shall pray for. Perhaps one is a CATALYST, multiplying the power of the other by thousands upon thousands of times. Certain it is that even Jesus, when those about Him were not in sympathy with Him and did not believe in Him, as on the occasion of His visit to Nazareth, worked no mighty works. Perhaps that is why, when He sent out His disciples to heal the sick, He sent them out "two by two."

Be that as it may, one thing is sure: If two or more of you will get together for a minute or two each day, and really agree as touching the thing you shall ask and the way you shall ask for it, you will get amazing results. Mind you, it is not enough to merely pray together for the same thing. You must unite your thought. You may ask me to pray with you that you may be healed of an ulcerated stomach, and when we pray, you may be picturing those sores and thinking of the pain and trouble they have been causing, while I am picturing the perfect organ that God gave you. That is not uniting our forces. That is setting them in opposition. We must both think health. We must both see in our mind's eye the thing we WANT—not the one we fear or wish to be rid of.

The same is true of debts. You may be thinking of all the money you owe, of the mortgage that is falling due, of the cut in pay you had to take, while I am trying to help you by thinking of the Infinite Supply that God is sending you. We'll never accomplish much that way. We've BOTH got to think of and visualize RICHES—not debts or lack. We've got to remember that the debts or other wrong conditions are merely the LACK of riches or health or other good thing, and that when we provide the good, the evil disappears as naturally as darkness disappears when you turn on the light. So what we must think of and see in our mind's eye is the light—i.e. the riches or the perfect health or the love or other good thing we desire.

If two can unite in doing that, there is no good thing they can ask, believing, that they cannot get. In the preceding chapter, we quoted the article by Elizabeth Gregg in "Nautilus," telling how five women prayed together, and every prayer was answered. And in Chapter Five, we told of a similar group in Russell Conwell's church who accomplished even more marvelous results through united prayer. You have problems too great to be solved by you alone. And you have friends with problems that they are unable to handle. Why not get together and unite your forces? Why not meet for fifteen minutes once a week, talk over your difficulties, decide upon the case that seems most pressing, and then at a certain time each day, all of you drop whatever you are doing and give a minute or two to uniting your thought and your prayers? You CAN do it, and you will be amazed at the power of your united prayers. There is nothing of good you can ask, believing, that cannot and will not be done for you.

> No *star is ever lost we once have seen.*
> *We always may be what we might have been.*

THE FIRST COMMANDMENT

If with pleasure you are viewing
 Anything a man is doing,
If you prize him, if you love him,
 Tell him now.
Don't withhold your approbation
 Until the Parson makes oration
And he lies with many lilies on his brow.

For no matter how you shout it
 He won't really know about it,
He won't count the many teardrops
 That you shed.
If you think some praise is due him,
 Now's the time to pass it to him.
For he cannot read his tombstone when he's dead.

What shall I do to be saved?" asked the rich young man of Jesus 1900 years ago. And today most of us are asking essentially the same question—"What shall I do to be saved from poverty and sickness and unhappiness, here and now as well as in the hereafter?"

"Keep the commandments!" was the Master's answer to the rich man. And later, when asked—"What is the greatest commandment," He told His hearers: "Thou shalt love the Lord thy God with all thy heart, and with all they soul, and with all thy mind: *This is the first and great commandment. And the second is like unto it. Thou shalt love thy neighbor as thyself.* On these two commandments hang all the Law and the Prophets."

Sounds simple enough, but just what is "loving God"? Is it going to Church and being a professed Christian? Or is it simply BEING THANKFUL AND HAPPY!

Going to Church and being an example to your neighbors is excellent, but is there any way in which you can show your love for God better than by being happy? Happiness implies praise, satisfaction with what God has done, thankfulness for His good gifts. Happiness means that you are enjoying life, appreciating it to the full, radiating joy to all about.

And loving your neighbor is just making him happy, too—praising him and blessing him and doing what you can to help him.

Can you think of any commandment, any law, that would do as much towards universal peace, towards settling the strife between labor and capital, towards bringing the millennium, as these two?

1. Be thankful and happy yourself.
2. Try to make your neighbor happy.

"On these two commandments hang all the Law and the Prophets."
Someone has wisely said that the first step towards universal peace is to have peace in our own hearts—to wish our neighbors well, to bless and praise even those who have used us despitefully. Evelyn Gage Browne expressed the thought when she wrote—

This old world needs the tender touch,
The kindly word, the lifting hand,
The love that blesses us so much,
And friendly hearts that understand.

It is said that a woman once went to Krishna and asked him how to find the love of God. "Who do you love most?" he inquired. "My brother's child," she answered. "Go back and love him more," advised Krishna. She did so, and lo! Behind the boy, she saw the form of the Christ child.

The same thought is expressed in the old legend of the group that went out to find the Christ child. There were knights and great ladies and monks and clergymen and all manner of people, and among the latter was a kindly old shoemaker. Everyone laughed at the idea of his going out when so many of the great ones of the earth were ahead of him. But after they had all come back disappointed, the bent little shoemaker walked joyfully in, accompanied by the Christ child himself.

"Where did you find Him?" they asked. And the Christ Child answered for him—"I hid myself in common things. You failed to find me because you did not look with the eyes of love."

Millions of books have been written about love, but most of them know not even the meaning of the word. To them, love is passion, self-gratification. Real love is not that. Real love is GIVING. It seeks only the good of the loved one. Yet in giving love freely, you get it, for it is like energy in that it expands only as it is released. It is like a seed in that it multiplies only when you sow it. As Ella Wheeler Wilcox put it—

Give love, and love to your heart will flow,
A strength in your utmost need;
Have faith and a score of hearts will show
Their faith in your word and deed.

Carlyle defined wealth as the number of things a man loves and blesses, which he is loved and blessed by.

Who are the unhappiest creatures on earth? Not the poor or the sick—but those who keep all their love for themselves. They may be worth millions, they may have dozens of servants to attend to their every want, but they are bored to extinction. They are miserable. Why? Because they have stopped giving, and as the words of a beautiful hymn express it—

For we must share, if we would keep
That blessing from above.
Ceasing to give, we cease to have—
Such is the Law of Love.

Life is expansion, mentally and physically. When you stop growing, you die. That is literally true in the case of your body cells, and figuratively true mentally, for when you cease to progress mentally, you are as good as dead. The undertaker may not call for a year or two, but so far as useful purposes are concerned, you might as well be buried.

And just as life is action, so is happiness service. For in helping and praising others and making them happy, you win happiness for yourself. Charles Kingsley once said that we knew our relations to God only through our relations with each other. No man can love God while he hates his neighbor. No man can love God while he is himself unhappy or deliberately makes another unhappy.

To be unhappy implies a criticism of God. An unhappy man cannot be grateful, he cannot be trustful, he cannot be at peace—and without these, how can he love God?

Yet if he lives only for himself, he is bound to be unhappy. "For whosoever shall save his life shall lose it," said the Master. "But whosoever shall lose his life for My sake, the same shall save it." He who loses himself in the service of others shall find therein life and love and happiness.

Longfellow tells of sending first an arrow into the air, and then a song, and seeming to lose them. But presently he found the arrow in an oak tree, and the song, from beginning to end, he found in the heart of a friend.

"He prayeth well," wrote Coleridge, "who loveth well both man and bird and beast.

> *He prayeth best, who loveth best*
> *All things both great and small;*
> *For the dear God who loveth us,*
> *He made and loveth all.*

When Jane Addams graduated from college, the doctors told her she had only six months to live. If a doctor told you that, what would you do? Most of us would simply sit down and die, and feel very sorry for ourselves in the doing of it.

Not so Jane Addams. "If I have only six months to live," she said, "I'll use those six months to do just as much as I can of the things I want most to do for humanity."

And she so lost herself in the work that she forgot to die. Eight years after the time predicted for her demise, she started Hull House, the Chicago settlement that is known the world over. Not only that, but her health was as good or better than that of the doctors who had prophesied her end.

Everyone has heard of Luther Burbank and of the marvelous success he had in growing things. He could take even a prickly cactus plant and from its shoots grow a plant without thorns or prickers, from which cattle could get sustenance on even the dryest soil.

How did he work such wonders with all manner of growing things? Through the magic of love! He blessed each little plant, he praised and nursed and loved it. And the life in it responded by giving him such results as no man before him had ever dreamed of. Here is the message that Luther Burbank sent to his friends on his last birthday:

As you hold loving thoughts toward every person and animal and even toward plants, stars, oceans, rivers and hills, and as you are helpful and of service to the world, so you will find yourself growing more happy each day, and with the happiness comes health and everything you want.

"Love and you shall be loved," said Emerson. "All love is mathematically just, as much as the two sides of an algebraic equation." The old philosopher who said—"Take out of life anything you want, *and pay for it,*" stated an eternal truth. You get as you give. It is well to remind one's self of this frequently by repeating now and then, when inclined to be disturbed by seeming difficulties—"I so love that I see all good and give all good, *and all good comes back to me.*"

The Magic Word

The most universal desire in all the world is man's natural desire for happiness. It is the purpose of existence. It is God's plan—to make man WIN happiness through struggle and service, through adding to the happiness of others.

Why is it that a moving-picture actor makes a thousand times as much as a teacher, or as an average business man or even a clergyman? Because he makes many thousand times as many people happy. He enables them to forget their troubles, to live their ideals, their dreams, through his picturing of them. When the rest of us find some way to make as many people happy, we shall share in like rewards.

A long time ago, Emerson wrote—"He who addresses himself to modes and wants that can be dispensed with, builds his house off the road. But he who addresses himself to problems every man must come to solve, builds $$$ house on the road, and every man must come to it."

Just ask yourself—What have I to GIVE that will add to the happiness of those around me? You will be surprised how many simple little ways of brightening the lives of others will present themselves, and how great the reward these ways can bring, when multiplied by hundreds or thousands.

A man down in Washington was too poor to buy his child toys, yet he wanted above everything to make that child happy. So with his pocket-knife, he carved out of discarded pieces of lumber a rough sort of Kiddie-car. It made such a hit, not only with his own youngster but with every child around, that he took it to a manufacturer and made a fortune out of it.

Years ago, a young veterinary over in England had a mother who was confined to a wheel chair. To soften the jolts for her, he fastened a strip of rubber around the iron tires. Those strips of rubber, through constant improvement, developed into the famous Dunlop tire, which have sold by the million.

There are similar stories to be found by the hundred. The only limit to your opportunities is the limit of human happiness. And that has not yet been reached.

"My husband died a short time ago," writes a poor, harassed widow, "leaving his estate so involved that it looks as though we shall lose everything. What can I do? I have two young children to clothe and feed and educate, and I've never made a penny in my life. Tell me, is it wrong to pray for death, for I don't know what else we can do?"

Is it wrong to pray for death? What do *you* think? Is praying for death showing love for God, confidence in Him? What did the Prophet of old, in similar case? "My husband is dead," wailed the widow to Elisha, "and the creditor is come to take unto him my two sons to be bondmen." Did Elisha demand that God rain down gold upon her? On the contrary—he asked what she had in the house, and with it he helped her to win her own salvation.

Read the story of Mary Elizabeth, and you will find an almost exact parallel. A widow with three children, no money, and the creditor "Poverty" demanding those children for bondservants. But the oldest of them asked herself—"What have we in the house?"—and found an ability to make others happy through delicious candy. Today the whole family is independently wealthy.

> *You have no talent? Say not so.*
> *A weaker brother you can lift*
> *And by your strength help him to go*
> *Renewed and blessed—this is your gift.*
>
> *No talent? Some one needs a word*
> *Of courage, kindness, love, and cheer—*
> *Which only you can speak—to gird*
> *His spirit against grief and fear.*
>
> *Yours is a special gift that none*
> *But you can use. Oh, lift your heart!*
> *So much of good will be undone*
> *Unless you do your own great part.*
>
> *You are God's helper day by day;*
> *He comforts, guides, and speaks through you;*
> *He needs just you in this blest way.*
> *No talent? Oh, that is not true!*
>
> —EVELYN GAGE BROWNE

The ancient Greeks had a legend that all things were created by love. Everyone was happy, because love was everywhere, and each vied with the other to make those around him happy.

Then one night while love slept, fear crept in, and with it came disease and lack and all unhappiness. For where love attracts, fear repels. Where love gives freely, fear is afraid there will not be enough for all, so holds on to everything it has.

What was the knowledge of good and evil against which God warned Adam in the Garden? Wasn't it a knowledge of things *to fear?*

In the second chapter of Genesis, we are told that Adam and Eve were naked and were not ashamed. Why? Because they knew no evil—therefore they feared no evil.

But they ate of the Tree of Knowledge of good and evil. They learned about evil. They hid themselves in the Garden in fear of evil. And immediately evil things began to happen to them, and have continued happening to their descendants ever since.

In the Garden of Eden, everything was abundance. The earth gave of its fruit bountifully. Then man learned fear. And having been given dominion over the earth, his fear reacted upon it. He feared it would hold back its fruits. He feared there would not be enough for all. He feared the snake and the wild animal, which before had been docile to his love.

What was the result? Instead of giving of its abundance gladly, he had to wrest its fruits from the earth. Instead of the luscious fruits and herbs of the Garden, the earth gave him the product of his fears—thorns and thistles. Instead of friendship between him and the beasts of the forest, there was the natural fruit of fear—suspicion and enmity.

From the time he ate of the Tree of Knowledge of Good and Evil, man has reaped the fruits of fear. And as long as his belief in evil holds, he will continue to reap the fruits of fear.

God is love. And what is the first characteristic of love? *To give.* God is constantly giving to us *all that we will accept.*

But that is, alas, woefully little. For the first characteristic of fear is to shut up every opening, whether of income or outgo. Fear repels. Fear holds on to what it has, lest it should be unable to get more. Fear takes only what it can grab. It will not open its doors and let good come in. It is too much afraid of evil.

The result is that good comes to us through fear only after great struggle and suffering, even though the good be all the time trying to manifest itself. It is like a fortress built upon the highest peak of a great mountain. It is so fearful of evil coming to it that it has put itself as far as possible away from good as well.

Love opens the petals of the flowers and the leaves of all growing things to the sun, giving freely of its fragrance, and thereby draws to itself every element it needs for growth and fruition.

Love asks—What have we in the house that will make others happy?—and thereby attracts to itself everything necessary for its own happiness.

What is the first and greatest commandment? To give out love, to make the world a happier place than you found it. Do that, and you cannot keep happiness from coming to you, too.

"I often wonder," says Andrew Chapman, "why people do not make more of the marvelous power there is in Kindness. It is the greatest lever to move the hearts of men that the world has ever known—greater by far than anything that mere ingenuity can devise, or subtlety suggest. Kindness is the kingpin of Success in life; it is the prime factor in overcoming friction and making the human machinery run smoothly. If a man is your enemy, you can not disarm him in any other way so surely as by doing him a kind act."

THE LADY OR THE TIGER

In ancient times, it is said that there lived a king whose methods of administering justice were original in the extreme.

He built a huge arena to seat himself and all his people. Under it, he put two doors. When a culprit was brought before him, accused of any crime, the king gave him his choice of which door he would open. If the accused man chose the right door, there came forth from it a beautiful lady, who was forthwith wed to him. But if he chose the wrong door, there came out of it a fierce and hungry tiger, which immediately tore him to pieces.

The king had a beautiful daughter, and upon a time it came to pass that a handsome young courtier fell in love with her and she with him. That was a grievous crime, for it did not at all suit the king's plans that his daughter should marry a commoner, no matter how well favored he might be. So the poor suitor was promptly clapped into a cell, and informed that on the morrow he must stand trial in the arena like any common culprit.

The princess was heartbroken. She tried prayers, she tried tears, but her father was adamant. Any common man who dared lift his eyes to her deserved death, and death he should have—death, or marriage to someone in his own station.

Failing to move her father, the princess tried the guards. But no amount of gold would persuade them to free her lover. This much she did accomplish, though—she learned from which door the tiger would come, from which the lady. More, she learned who the lady was, and horror of horrors, it was one she had seen more than once casting amorous glances at her lover!

The morning found her torn between love and jealousy. She could not see her lover killed before her eyes—and yet, would it not be better to suffer that moment of agony, and be able to remember him as loving only her, than to see him day after day in the arms of another, see the triumph in that other's eyes, see his own eyes turn away from her to the beauty in his arms?

As in a dream, she took her place on the dais at her father's right hand. As in a dream, she saw her lover step forth, saw him look to her for a sign, saw herself signal to him to choose the right hand door—then hid her face that she might see no more.

Which had she chosen—the Lady or the Tiger? Which would you choose in like circumstances? Judging from the newspapers of the day, all too many, even in our so-called civilization, would choose the tiger. Why? Because they would rather see their lover dead than in the arms of another. Their idea of love is passion, self-gratification, and if they can't have their loved one for themselves, they don't want anyone else to have him, regardless of how he or the other may suffer.

At some time and in one modified form or another, that choice of the Lady or the Tiger comes to most people, and your answer depends solely upon what kind of love yours is. If it is real love, you will not hesitate for a moment, for real love is selfless and free from all fear. (And that is all jealousy is—*fear!*) Real love gets its happiness from giving. It lavishes itself upon the object of its affections without thought of return. And by its very prodigality, it brings back real love to itself.

For love is a magnet. Like the magnet of iron which gives off electricity, by its very giving it draws to itself its own. And again like the iron magnet, when its strength is done, when all power has gone out of it, it has only to rub against a stronger magnet to be renewed!

What is it that makes men and women fall in love? Not beauty; that attracts attention. But love requires more than beauty. Love requires personality, *charm*, MAGNETISM!

And what is magnetism? What but the power you GIVE OUT! It is vitality, it is abounding interest in people and things, it is LOVE!

You cannot be self-centered and still give out magnetism. You cannot think only of the gratification of your own desires and still expect to win or hold another's love.

Love gives out a current of love, and all who come within its aura are attracted to it. Selfishness, jealousy, hate, are like layers of insulation around a magnet. They not only shut off all love from going out, but they keep any from getting in. A selfish man, a jealous man, an angry man, has no magnetism. He repels everyone he comes in contact with. He has shut off his own current, and insulated himself against any from the outside.

I remember reading a story of a man who had become involved in a serious law-suit. He was bitter and resentful, for he felt that his opponents had been most unfair and unjust. But the suit was apparently going against him.

He went to a teacher of the mental sciences and laid his case before him. The teacher told him he would never get anywhere with his case until he rid himself of his resentment and hatred. "Bless your opponents," he advised. "Know that in some way not yet apparent they are doing you a favor. Say to yourself, whenever thoughts of resentment creep in—'I live by the law of love.' And then try to do just that."

The man tried it, and found that he could not keep saying and using this affirmation without its affecting everything he did. There came a most unexpected opportunity to do a great favor for his opponents. Reluctantly he did it, and lo and behold, it opened the way to a fair settlement of the whole case—a settlement that proved eventually far more profitable to him than winning the case would have done.

"Doubt not, fear not, work on and wait; as sure as dawn shall conquer dark, so love will triumph over hate." So writes Douglas Malloch, and in a recent issue of "Nautilus" magazine, Sonia Shand tells of a "Love Game" which bears out the same idea.

It is based, she says, on Shakespeare's "Taming of the Shrew." You remember, in the play, no matter what Katharine said or did, Petruchio acted as though she were falling in with his wishes, and the more contrary she became, the more he would praise her for her sweet submission to his every wish. Well, this game is as simple as that. No matter what happens during the time you are playing your game of Love, you smile and say it is good and wonderful.

Whether a feared bill collector comes blustering to your door, or the neighbors' children pull up your favorite flowers, or any one of the hundred annoying things that are part of your daily existence happen, just smile and give thanks for them as though they were great blessings instead of annoying trials.

Release the feeling of love toward each and every annoying thing as though it were the best that ever happened to you. You will be amazed at the results that come from this little game, because in love, no matter how tiny the grain of it, there is unlimited power for good, and it is never wasted.

You have heard the old adage that a soft answer turneth away wrath. This game has the same principle incorporated in it, with a lot more added to it. Nonresistance is one thing, but by itself it is negative. Add your praise and blessings to it, and you turn it into a positive force for good.

To love all things is our natural heritage. It was what made Adam and Eve so happy in the Garden of Eden. The snake of Fear crept into their hearts and turned them out of Eden, but we can each of us get back in if we will use the game of Love.

Try it. And while you are playing it, be sure to glorify *yourself*. See yourself as the perfect individual you always had hoped some day to become. Be the charming, gracious, noble self, who is raised by the powers of Love to a level above all sordid, petty, annoying and ugly things of life. Be that for one hour each day, and you will be amazed how quickly you will be that all the day.

You can use this Love Game in the home, in business, in whatever you are doing and wherever you are working.

If you are a business man, perhaps worried by a heavy load of debts and obligations, bless your creditors with the thought of abundance as you begin to accumulate the wherewithal to pay off your obligations. Keep the faith they had in you by including them in your prayer for increase. Begin to free yourself at once by doing all that is possible with the means you have, and as you proceed in this spirit the way will open for you to do more. For through the avenues of Spirit, more means will come to you and every obligation will be met.

If you are a creditor, be careful of the kind of thoughts you hold over your debtor. Avoid the thought that he is unwilling to pay you or that he is unable to pay you. One thought holds him to be dishonest and the other holds him to be subject to lack, and either of them tends to close the door to the possibility of his paying you soon.

Declare abundant supply for both creditors and debtors, and thus help them to prosper. Pray and work for their good as well as for your own, for yours is inseparable from theirs. You owe your debtor quite as much as he owes you and yours is a debt of love. Pay your debt to him and he will pay his to you.

Take anything in your life that seems not to be going well, and give a few minutes each day to "treating" it. Remind yourself first that harmony and true success are the Divine purpose of your life, that there are no exceptions to this law, therefore this particular difficulty must come under it. That being so, this thing that troubles you cannot be inharmonious or negative, once you know the truth about it. Know, therefore, the truth must be that in some way this difficulty is working out for your good, that beneath its hard and ugly outer shell, there is a kernel of perfect good for you. So bless the good within.

How does the kernel of the black walnut break its tough shell and send up a green shoot that presently grows into a great tree? By heating within! And that is the way you have to break the shell of every difficulty and trial that confronts you—by BLESSING the kernel of good you know to be within it, by praising and loving it until it expands and bursts its shell and springs forth as the fragrant plant of good for you.

Praise, blessing, thanksgiving, LOVE—these will solve any difficulty, tame any shrew of sickness or trouble. Start each day by saying—"This is the day which Jehovah hath made; I will rejoice and be glad in it. I thank God for abundant life, I thank God for enduring love. I thank God for joy, I thank God for glorious health, I thank God for infinite supply. I have awakened to a new day. I join the birds and all created things in glorious praise and thanksgiving. Lord, I do give Thee thanks for the abundance that is mine."

> *If I have faltered more or less*
> *In my great task of happiness;*
> *If I have moved among my race*
> *And shown no glorious morning face;*
> *If beams from happy human eyes*
> *Have moved me not; if morning skies,*
> *Books and my food, and summer rain*
> *Knocked on my sullen heart in vain;*
> *Lord, Thy most pointed pleasure take*
> *And stab my spirit broad awake.*
> —ROBERT LOUIS STEVENSON

EXERCISE FOR CHAPTER THIRTEEN

Remember, in "Vanity Fair," the owner of a fine estate who always carried acorns in his pocket, and when strolling about his grounds, if he came to a vacant spot, he would dig a little hole with his foot and drop an acorn into it. "An acorn costs nothing," he was fond of saying, "but it may spread into a prodigious bit of timber."

The same is true of words of praise, of blessing. They cost nothing, but when planted in the waste places of human consciousness, they become tremendously productive of happiness. As Willa Hoey expressed it—

> *It's the little things we do and say*
> *That mean so much as we go our way.*
> *A kindly deed can lift a load*
> *From weary shoulders on the road,*
> *Or a gentle word, like summer rain,*

*May soothe some heart and banish pain.
What joy or sadness often springs
rom just the simple, little things!*

Write it on your heart that each day is the best day of the year. There is no tomorrow, you know; there is no yesterday. There is only the eternal NOW. So make the most of your happiness *now*, while you can.

You create your own environment, so only YOU are to blame if some existing situation seems unhappy. That being so, only YOU can rectify it. You must cure it in your own thought before it can be remedied anywhere else. "Nothing is evil, but thinking makes it so."

Instead of thinking unhappy thoughts, sickly thoughts, thoughts of poverty and lack, talk to the God in You about the good things you want. Start with what you have, and suggest to him each day that you are getting stronger, healthier, richer, happier. Talk to Him as to a rich and loving Father, describing the improvements you see in your affairs, the finer body you have in your mind's eye, the more important work you should be doing, the lovelier home, the richer rewards. Talk them over for ten minutes each day when you are alone with Him. You will be amazed at how readily He will help you to carry out your suggestions.

Don't worry about how He is to bring about the conditions you desire. Just talk to Him confidently, serenely, happily—and then leave the rest to Him. And for your prayers, here is an affirmation used by Unity which has been found unusually effective:

"My Father-God, I place all my dependence in Thee, Thou giver of every good and perfect gift. Thou who art the source of my being art also the source of my supply. All that I shall ever need is in Thy mind for me, prepared for me from the beginning. Omnipresent substance, the garment with which Thou clothest Thy universe, with which Thou nourishest all Thy creation, is also mine to have and to use for my every desire and for the blessing of others of Thy children. I open myself fully through my faith in Thee, through my vision of Thy abundance, through my expectancy of its manifestation for me. I open my hands, my pocketbook, my wardrobe, my business, my bank account, and from Thy rich storehouse Thou dost fill every vessel that I hold out to Thee full to overflowing with Thine own omnipresent good and in Thine own good measure, pressed down, shaken together, running over. I thank

Thee, my Father-God, that through the Christ in me I can touch Thine omnipresent substance and all my world be clothed with Thy opulence. I praise and give thanks that now and throughout eternity I am one with Thee and that in this union all Thine is mine and mine is Thine forever and ever."

Throughout this book, we shall give you numbers of affirmations to use for different conditions. Don't try to use them all at once. Use one until it becomes so familiar that you find yourself repeating it too parrotlike. Then change to another. All are helpful. The mere statement—"I am good," "I am strong," "I am capable," is an upbuilding affirmation that tends to start your subconscious trying to bring about that condition in you, just as negative statements such as "I am poor or sick" tend to make those conditions true. So try to remember always to PRAISE God in every thing and every condition that confronts you. Praise Him and look for the Divinity in each.

Praise God that Good is everywhere;
Praise to the Love we all may share—
The Life that thrills in you and me;
Praise to the Truth that sets us free.

THE THREE LAWS OF LIFE

For thousands of years, philosophers have wrangled over the problem of why men without scruple or conscience should so often succeed, while good men of equal ability fail. Some tell us it is because the wicked have their innings in this world and will suffer for it through eternity, while we shall have our turn at happiness and plenty then. That is a bit unsatisfying, especially when those near and dear to us are suffering for lack of things we should be able to give them. But for many, it has to suffice.

But not for all! A few have learned that there are definite laws governing success—just as definite and just as certain of results as the laws of Physics.

These basic laws govern everything you do. They rule all of mankind, whether mankind likes it or not. They are unlike man-made laws in that they govern high and low alike. They defer neither to rich nor to poor, to weak nor to powerful—only to those with an understanding heart. It was with them in mind that the wisest of ancient kings bade us seek first understanding, and all things else would be added to us. Summed up, those laws are:

1. *The Law of Averages,* under which man in the mass is no better off than the animals, his chances of happiness and success in life but little better than one in a hundred.

2. *The Law of Tendency,* which is towards Life-GIVING. To the extent that a man allies himself with this great fundamental force of nature, to that extent he improves his chances for success.

3. *The Law of Capillary Attraction,* which gives to every nucleus the power to draw to itself those things necessary for its growth and fulfillment. It is through this third law that man is able to rise above the Law of Averages. It is by using it with the Law of Tendency that he is able to reach any height, attain any goal.

Under the Law of Averages, man in the mass is subject to alternate feast or famine, happiness or misery—just as the animals are. Nature seems carelessly profligate. She brings forth enough fish to choke the sea—then lets the many die that the few may live. She gives life with a prodigal hand— then seems entirely careless of it, letting the mass suffer or perish so long as the few survive.

To man she has given inexhaustible riches—but the few have most of it while the many toil to serve them.

That is Nature's Law of Averages in the animal kingdom. That is Nature's Law of Averages for man in the mass. But for man the individual she reserves a different fate.

As long as he chooses to be governed by the Law of Averages, man must be content with his one chance in a hundred of prosperity and happiness. But let him separate himself from the mass, and he can choose his own fate.

And the way to separate himself from the mass is—not to journey to some desert or forgotten isle, not to mew himself up in a solitary cell—but to hitch his wagon to the star of some strong purpose, and thereby pull himself out of the mass of self-centered, self-seeking, merely animal humanity, and ally himself with the great fundamental Law of the Universe, which carries all mankind upon its crest.

The word "Man," you know, means steward or distributor. The purpose of man here on earth is to utilize and distribute God's good gifts. To the extent that he cooperates in this purpose, he is allying himself with the forces behind all of nature. To the extent that he looks out only for his own selfish ends, he is opposing it. "I came," said Jesus, "that they might have life, and have it more abundantly." And He demonstrated His mission by giving more of life to all who sought it.

And what is "Life"? Life is energy. Life is power. Life is supply. Life is the creative force out of which the world and everything in it was made in the beginning, and is made now.

As I see Him, God is the Life-Principle which permeates and directs the universe. His "sons" are the individual subconscious minds or Spiritual Selves back of each of us, pouring Life into us, guiding and governing (to the extent we permit them) all the complicated functions of our bodies, all our outward circumstances and conditions.

These "sons" are like vast Genii, possessing all riches, all happiness, all wisdom on their own plane, but forced to reflect those God-like gifts upon the material plane only as we (their mirrors) can understand and express them.

They pour their Life-Energy through us in a continuous stream, like the strips of steel that are fed into stamping machines in a steel mill. Going in, it is potential life, potential power, potential riches. But like the strips of steel, coming out it is only what we have expressed through it— what our stamping machine (our innermost beliefs) has impressed upon it.

Whatever we truly believe, whatever we love and bless and hold constantly in thought as our own, it brings into being in our lives, in our bodies, in our circumstances. Like light shining through a prism it is broken up into its component colors in passing through our conscious minds. But like the prism, our minds can be darkened by fear and worry to shut off all the happier colors. It is a perfect stream of Life-Energy that starts through us, but just as a poorly made die in a stamping machine can cut crude and ugly patterns on the best of steel, just as a faulty prism can turn beams of sunshine into shadows, so can your beliefs turn perfect Life-Energy into manifestations of sickness and poverty and misery. God does not inflict them upon you—you do.

The first essential, then, is to change the pattern—to watch your beliefs as the Director of the U. S. Mint watches the molds which cast the coins he turns out. Instead of picturing the things you FEAR, and thus stamping their mold upon the Life-Energy passing through you, picture the conditions you WANT. "What things soever ye ask for when ye pray," said Jesus, "believe that ye RECEIVE them, and ye shall HAVE them!"

What do YOU want? Know that your spiritual self HAS it. Like the perfect flower in the tiny unopened bud, it is all there, needing only the sunshine of your faith to bring it forth.

You have seen trees in the winter, all the twigs bare, with no sign of the brilliant foliage soon to spring from them. Yet the leaves are already there, perfectly formed, waiting only for the warm sunshine to bring them out. In the same way, the things YOU want are already around you, no matter how bare everything may look. They need only the sunshine of your faith to bring them forth.

That is the first step, *to have faith!* That is the pattern which molds all your circumstances—*your beliefs.* Get that pattern right. It is there that unscrupulous men get ahead of their less understanding brethren. Knowingly or unknowingly, they have hit upon the fact that the first essential of material success is to believe in themselves, believe that the world belongs to them, believe that it *owes* them a living. They may not knowingly BLESS the things they want, but they LOVE them, long for them, put them above everything else in life, and since God is love, it sometimes seems that we have only to love a thing greatly to get it.

To that extent, they are right. Their trouble is that they do not bother to look around for right sources from which to draw their supply. They take whatever is not nailed down, and sooner or later they run afoul of the Law of Tendency and end in ruin.

This Law of Tendency is our next step, for it *requires co-operation* with the Life-Giving forces of the universe— *swimming with the tide.*

The Law of Tendency is based upon the fact that the whole purpose of Life is growth. The forces of nature are Life-GIVING forces. Its fundamental trends are towards the advancement of life, the good of the world. Those businesses and those individuals whose work is in line with that tendency are swept forward by the great tide of good. Those whose work tends to hinder the forward movement of life are sooner or later brushed aside and cast upon the rocks.

Ella Wheeler Wilcox expressed the thought beautifully when she wrote—The world has a thousand creeds, and never a one have I, Nor church of my own, though a million spires are pointing the way on high.

But I float on the bosom of faith, that bears me along like a river:

And the lamp of my soul is alight with love, for life, and the world and the Giver.

"But," I can hear you say, "I know many worthy men whose efforts were always for good, yet who are hopeless failures." True—but so do I know many swimmers who cannot keep afloat a hundred yards, even with the strongest tide behind them. The tide is the second step. The first step is to get your pattern right—in other words, learn how to swim. And having the tide with you makes that first step none the less necessary.

Believe in yourself. Look upon yourself as one of the Lords of the Universe. Know that it belongs to you. BELIEVE THAT YOU *HAVE* the things you want. Love them. Bless them. Thank God for them, even before they seem manifest. "Lord, I do give Thee thanks for the abundance that is mine."

That is the first essential. The second is to USE your powers for good—*get on the side of the* Life-GIVING *forces*.

"Sounds well," perhaps you will say, "but I'd like you to tell me how I am going to use riches for good, when my principal reason for taking this course is to learn how to GET riches to keep the wolf from my own door!"

The first essential in the creation of anything—be it a house or an automobile or a fortune—is the mental picture or image. Before God made man, He "imaged" him—He formed a mental picture of him. Then He poured His Life-Energy into that image, and it became man. Before an architect builds a house, he draws a mental picture of it, he "images" it upon paper. Then he pours materials and energy into that image and it becomes a house. Before you can build a fortune, you must form it in your mind's eye. You must "image" it on the mental plane, and in that mental image you must think of it as already yours. In other words, "believe that you HAVE it!" An easy way to do this is the "Treasure Mapping" outlined in Chapter 10.

One of the startling facts of modern science is that this universe is not a finished product. Creation is going on all around us—new worlds being formed, cosmic energy taking shape in a million different molds.

But a far more startling fact to most of us is that WE ARE CREATORS, and that we can form today the world we personally shall be living in tomorrow.

People blame their environment, their education, their opportunities, their luck, for their condition. They are wrong. There is one person to blame—and only one— THEMSELVES. They are today the result of their thoughts of yesterday and the many yesterdays that preceded it. They are forming today the mold for what they will be in the years to come.

For there is no such thing as failure. Whether you are poor and sickly, or rich and strong, you have succeeded in one thing. You have compressed the cosmic energy about you into the mold that you held before the mind's eye of your inner self. You have named the forces that worked with you "good" or "bad," and as you named them, so have they been to you as servants—Good, or Evil.

But there is a happy ending. You don't need to leave things as they are. If you don't like the present results you can rename those servants. You can bless and praise the good, no matter how tiny it may seem, and by your praise and blessing, you can expand it a thousand-fold.

Which brings us to the third step—"The Law of Capillary Attraction."

Plant a seed of corn in the ground, and it will attract to itself from the earth and the water and the air everything it needs for its growth. Plant the seed of a desire in your mind and it forms a nucleus with power to attract to itself everything needed for its fulfillment. But just as the seed of corn needs sunshine and air and water from which to draw the energies necessary to bring forth the perfect ear, so does your seed of desire need the sunshine of a perfect faith, the fruitful soil of a will-power held steadfast to the one purpose.

This is the Alpha and Omega of all accomplishment— that every seed has in it the perfect plant, that every right desire has in it the perfect fulfillment, for Desire is God's opportunity knocking at your door. The seed must be planted, it must have nourishment and sunshine. The desire must be definitely planted by the work of starting the initial step in its accomplishment, it must be nourished by a will-power which holds it to its purpose, and it must have the warm sunshine of perfect faith. Given these, it will attract to itself whatever else is necessary to its fulfillment.

You see, the Law of Capillary Attraction is based upon the principle of growth from the vitality inherent in the seed or idea itself. It is like a snowball which starts with only a handful of snow, yet by gathering to itself all it comes in contact with, ends as an avalanche!

First the seed, the desire. Next, the planting—the initial step necessary to start its accomplishment. Third, the cultivation—the continual working towards the one end. You can't just WILL a thing into existence, you know. But you can use the will as the machinist uses a vise—to hold the tool of your purpose until it accomplishes its end. Fourth, the sunshine—FAITH—without which all the others are as nothing. Without sunshine, the seed will rot in the ground, the plant will wither on the stalk. Without faith, your desire will die still-born. Believe that you RECEIVE. See the perfect plant in the seed. See the perfect accomplishment in the desire.

Prof. Wm. James of Harvard, the greatest psychologist this country has known, wrote—"If you only care enough for a result, you will almost certainly attain it. If you wish to be rich, you will be rich; if you wish to be learned, you will be learned; if you wish to be good, you will be good. Only you must, then, really wish these things, and wish them exclusively, and not wish at the same time a hundred other incompatible things just as strongly."

But be careful that your desire tends towards Life-GIVING, towards the furtherance of Good. You can't make much of a snowball pushing up hill. If you do, it will presently grow bigger than you, get beyond your control, and engulf you in the resultant catastrophe. The fruit you bring forth is going to partake of the same nature as the seed you plant. If there is no kindliness in the seed, no love of your fellow-man, nothing but self-gratification, the fruit of your tree will be the same kind. It will be bitter to others—it will turn bitter in your own mouth.

Now how does this apply to you? There are certain things you want from life—Success, Riches, Fame, Honor, Love, Happiness, Health, Strength. All of these are worthy desires. All of them are entirely possible of fulfillment for you. How are you to go about getting them?

Your job here on earth is to distribute certain God-given gifts—certain goods, certain services, certain abilities—to the end that the world may be more livable for your having been in it.

In ancient Egypt, it was believed that each person was given at birth a "Ka" or "Double," which was his REAL SELF. It had infinite power for good. The body was merely its reflection, seen through the glass of the conscious mind.

So it is with you. Your REAL Self is God's image of you—the God in You. He gave it dominion over all the earth. Can you imagine it, then, as powerless under any circumstances, as poverty-stricken, as in doubt where its supply is coming from?

If you believe in God at all, you must believe in His intelligence. And if He is intelligent, He made nothing without a purpose. Everything fits into His plan. YOU, for instance—He created you for the purpose of performing certain work. That being so, it would seem pretty certain that He gave you every ability, every means necessary for the perfect performance of that work, would it not?

But how are you to know what that work is? Easily enough, if you stop to analyze your ambitions and desires. They are your subconscious promptings. Not, of course, the merely selfish desires for the gratification of some personal vanity or passion. But the big, deep down ambitions that come to you in exalted moments. They are the promptings of The God in You, urging you to EXPRESS on the material plane the work he is already doing in the mental realm.

You have an idea, let us say, which will short-cut the work of the world, make life easier and happier for any number of its inhabitants. You take whatever steps seem good to you to accomplish that idea. But you presently reach a point where lack of money or lack of knowledge or other circumstances leave you high and dry—seemingly at your rope's end. What are you to do then?

PRAY! And how are you to pray? Jesus gave us the formula—"Whatsoever things ye ask for when ye pray, believe that ye RECEIVE them, and ye shall HAVE them."

But how can you believe that you HAVE when you are at the end of your resources and there is no possible way out in sight? How? By knowing that The God in You, your REAL SELF, already HAS the answer in the realm of the REAL. By seeing the finished result there, imaging it in your mind's eye, and then putting it up to that God in You to show you the next step necessary to reflect that result on the material plane, in the serene confidence that, since he has worked out the answer, the EXPRESSION of it step by step through you is simple.

Tell yourself—and KNOW—you ARE rich, you ARE successful, you ARE well and happy and possessed of every good thing you desire. Use your "Treasure Map" to picture these things—then believe that you HAVE them.

No matter how limited your education, no matter how straitened your circumstances, the God in You HAS the knowledge and the means and the power to accomplish any right thing you may desire. Give him a job—and it is DONE! You HAVE it! And you have only to see that finished result in your mind's eye—"BELIEVE THAT YOU RECEIVE"—in order to begin to reflect it on the material plane.

Therein lies the nucleus of every success—the nucleus which has such life that it draws to itself everything it needs for its full expression—*the belief that you* HAVE. It is the secret of power, the Talisman of Napoleon. To acquire it takes just three things.

1. Know that this is a world of Intelligence. Nothing merely happens. You were put here for a purpose, and you were given every qualification and every means necessary to the accomplishment of that purpose. So you need never fear whether you are big enough, or smart enough, or rich enough to do the things required of you. "The Father knoweth that ye have need of these things," so do the things that are given you to do in the serene knowledge that your needs will be met.

2. Know that The God in You which is your REAL Self is already DOING this work you were given to do, so all that is required of you is to SEE that accomplished result, and REFLECT it step by step on the material plane, as the way is opened to you. "And thine ears shall hear a word behind thee, saying—This is the way. Walk ye in it."

3. Have serene faith in your God's ability to express the finished results through you. When you can SEE that result in your mind's eye as already accomplished, you will realize that you don't need to fear or worry or rush in and do things foolishly. You can go serenely ahead and do the things that are indicated for you to do. When you seem to reach a cul-de-sac, you can wait patiently, leaving the problem to The God in You in the confident knowledge that at the right time and in the right way he will give you a "lead" showing what you are to do.

The fundamental Law of the Universe, you remember, is the Law of Attraction. You attract to you whatever you truly love and bless and believe is YOURS.

Knowing that The God in You Has the fruition of your desire—knowing that the perfect leaf is in the bare twig of your present circumstances—it is easy to pour such life, love and blessings into that leaf that it bursts its bonds and blossoms forth for all to see.

So, like the Egyptians of old, let us commune with The God in Us night and morn, much as our reflection in the mirror might commune with us:

Reality of me, I greet you and salute you the perfect "me" God created. You have a perfect body, made in the image and likeness of God. Make that perfect body manifest in me. You have infinite riches—dominion over all things. Use that dominion, I pray you, to uncover and bring out in my life, my work and my surroundings the perfect reflection of (whatever your particular desire may be).

Then SEE, in your mind's eye, The God in You doing those things you wish to do, emphasizing the traits you wish to cultivate, displaying the riches or possessions you want. Know that he HAS these. And that as soon as you can SEE them through the prism of your conscious mind, as fast as you can *realize* their possession, *you, too, will reflect them for all the world to see!*

OUR PRAYERS ARE ANSWERED
BY BONNIE DAY

Our prayers are answered: each unspoken thought
And each desire implanted in the mind
Bears its own harvest, after its own kind;
Who dreams of beauty has already caught
The flash of angel wings. Who seeks to find
True wisdom shall assuredly be taught.
But thorns of fate have thorny thoughts behind;
For out of our own hearts our lives are wrought.

Be on thy guard, my soul, lest wind-blown seed
Into the fertile soil of thought should fall
And lodging place within the garden wall
Be given to bitter rue or noxious weed.
Unspoken prayers bear fruitage.
Love thoughts call Forth into being every loving deed.
Idle or earnest, still our prayers are all
Answered according to our inward creed.

A PRAYER FOR WORK

Lord give me work. All work is Thine.
Help me to make Thy business mine.
Give me my part, and let me share
Thy joy in making life more fair;
My part, and with the part the will
To make my life Thy plan fulfill.
Thus every day, Lord, help me see
My simplest task as done for Thee.
—ESTHER ANN CLARK

All day long and every day, the God in You keeps repeating—"I AM." But He lets YOU end the sentence. You can add "poor" or "rich," "sad" or "happy," "sick" or "well," as YOU choose. God can do for you only what you ALLOW Him to do THROUGH you. You praise and bless Him, only when you see the good and true and beautiful. You dishonor Him when you call yourself weak or sick or poor.

So claim the good! Praise God for it, thank Him and bless Him for all His good gifts.

If you are out of work at the moment, know that the Spirit of the Lord is upon you, directing you to your right work. The Spirit of God goes before you to make plain your way. It works through you to make you efficient, successful, prosperous and of real worth to your employer and associates.

Know this—and then open your channels! Give of what you have of service to others. Start where you are. Distant fields always look greener, but opportunity lies right where you are. Take advantage of every opportunity of service, even if it be only to wash dishes or do chores around your own home. Show God that you are a channel for good NOW The more you can prove that, the greater will be your opportunities, and soon those opportunities will take the form of just the right job for you.

Each night and morning, and whenever the need for a job occurs to you, repeat this affirmation:

"God in me knows what my right work is, where it is and what I ought to do to be actually engaged in it. Let this knowledge be quickened in me as a revelation to my conscious mind so I shall know what is my right work, where it is and what there is for me to do to be established in it."

Remember it is from within, and not from without, that you get in touch with all of Good. Every ill, every lack, every discordant condition, must be cured in your own thought first. It is like a radio. The programs of all the world are in the air about you, but you have to tune in on the one you want. When you turn on the radio, the program that comes to you may be some sordid tale of crime or unhappiness, or it may be merely static noises. If so, that is all you will get—until you turn the dial. But you CAN get the program you want, if you keep turning away from the others and persistently try until you find the one you want.

But you must both affirm and ACT the part. To affirm prosperity and then act like a pauper with what substance you have is to show that you do not believe your own affirmation and do not expect anything from it. It doesn't matter if you have to force yourself to take some appropriate action. Take it—and thereby increase your faith.

Every affirmation should be matched by some action expressing the faith that you HAVE received or ARE receiving, action of the sort you would engage in if the affirmed good were visibly and tangibly present.

That doesn't mean you must spend a lot of money recklessly, buy a lot of things such as you will when you have the riches you crave. It does mean you must take the mental attitude of BEING rich, HAVING the right sort of job, sprucing up, being confident and serene and unworried.

You can help others get the sort of place they want in the same way you can yourself. Here is an affirmation to use for others:

Infinite Spirit, open the way for So-and-so's right position (or home or abundance or what-not), the position he is best fitted to fill, the position that needs him and which no one else can fill so well as he. Let him be led to the right people, the right place where he can give good service for good pay. Lead him to make the right contacts. I leave it with you, and I know all is well.

In a recent issue of "Nautilus" magazine, Dortch Campbell tells how he prayed for a home—and found the one he had always dreamed of.

"The whole secret," he says, "lies in that beautiful thing called love. I prayed for a home. Every element in the answer that came was in accord with justice. The quality of love was not strained.

A house that you can call your own home is not so easy to obtain these days. For me it was most difficult. Conditions have been serious in the Mississippi Valley for nearly a decade; the cotton problem has become acute. But the house where I had lived for a long time was taken away from me. I was homeless; there was no other available, for people have not been building houses in my country.

I had to build my own home to find a roof for myself and my loved ones. But there was no mortal way to build that home. I had not sufficient money to buy even a lot. Yet the home of my own became a reality in answer to my prayers as simply and as unostentatiously as a rose unfolds.

I felt that we are far too selfish in our prayers, so I prayed for others when I prayed for myself. I asked that the contractor who should build my home should be blessed through me. I prayed for the owner of the land. I prayed for an harmonious association with the contractor. I asked that there be love and friendship between us and between all who might be associated in the undertaking. I prayed that he might find a way to finance my home and that I in turn should help him to succeed. I prayed for others as earnestly as I prayed for myself. I prayed for the landowners that they, through me, might sell other lots.

I prayed in this fashion, loving them that they in turn might love me. Deep within me, I desired that all of us might equally profit in the building of my home. This was all. There was no domination on my part, no attempt to influence or control them, no direct thought to them.

Step by step, that home came about. I obtained the lot for a very small outlay—a lot worth three times what I paid. The contractor himself actually gave me the money I required. The home became mine in such a gentle fashion that I, accustomed to prayer, stand amazed. Things— for example—like a driveway, were contributed free.

But it was not only I who was helped, and this to me is the most beautiful part of the answer to that prayer. It has been my privilege since the house was constructed to help those who helped me in getting my home. More lots have been sold, more will be sold. The contractor has closed several contracts as a result of building my home.

What we need is to be not only hearers but DO-ERS of the Word. We find Truth by trying to live it. Since God is love, it may be that we have only to love a thing greatly to get it. Can it be that the long-lost key to attainment through prayer is in feeling the loving power of God within to give us that which the heart desires?

> *If I can do some good today,*
> *If I can serve along life's way,*
> *If I can something helpful say,*
>   *Lord, show me how.*

> *If I can right a human wrong,*

The Magic Word

If I can help to make one strong,
If I can cheer with smile or song,
   Lord, show me how.

If I can make a burden less,
If I can aid one in distress,
If I can spread more happiness,
   Lord, show me how.

If I can do a kindly deed,
If I can sow a fruitful seed,
If I can help someone in need,
   Lord, show me how.

If I can feed a hungry heart,
If I can give a better start,
If I can fill a nobler part,
   Lord, show me how.

—GRENVILLE KLEISER

FIRST CAUSES

How can I tell if I am working a-right?"—many students ask us. And "How can I be sure I am following correct lines?"—is the question in the mind of many a man and woman when confronted by some unusual problem.

In his Edinburgh Lectures, Judge Troward gave so clear an answer to this question that I quote it here:

If we regard the fulfillment of our purpose as contingent upon any *circumstances*, past, present, or future, we are not making use of First Cause. We have descended to the level of *Secondary Causation*, which is the region of doubts, fears and limitations.

What is First Cause? Judge Troward defined it, too.

If a lighted candle is brought into a room, the room becomes illuminated; if the candle is taken away, it becomes dark again. Now the illumination and the darkness are both conditions, the one positive resulting from the presence of the light, the other negative resulting from its absence. From this simple example we therefore see that every positive condition has an exactly opposite negative condition corresponding to it, and that this correspondence results from their being related to the same cause, the one positively and the other negatively; and hence we may lay down the rule that all positive conditions result from the active presence of a certain cause, and all negative conditions from the absence of such a cause. A condition, whether positive or negative, is never primary cause, and the primary cause of any series can never be negative, for negation is the condition which arises from the absence of active causation.

How can you be sure that you are working a-right? By asking yourself one question: "On what am I putting my dependence for the riches, or the health, or the success I am seeking?" If the answer is—"Upon my ability, or my doctor, or his drugs, or the help of my friends," then you can rate your chances of success as not more than one in ten, for you are working with secondary causes, and secondary causes are always undependable.

But if your answer is—"I am throwing everything I have into my work, but I am putting my dependence for success—NOT on these *means*—but on the unquenchable, irresistible power of the Seed of Life working through me," why then you can count your chances of success as nine out of ten.

You see, it all comes back to the Fundamental Law of the Universe—that each nucleus, each seed, contains within itself vitality enough to draw to it every element it needs for its complete growth and fruition.

The Magic Word

But the seed must germinate, the nucleus must start whirling, before either has the slightest attractive power. Until they do that, they are so much congealed life, with no more "pull" to them than any other bit of inanimate matter around them.

Suppose you want something badly—more than anything else life can offer you at the moment. The desire for that something forms a nucleus, a seed, and like every other seed, it has latent in it the power to draw to itself the elements necessary for its complete growth and fruition. But until you *do* something about it, it is an inanimate nucleus, a seed that has not been planted, a nucleus with no power of attraction because no one has taken the trouble to start it whirling.

How can you put it to work? By PLANTING your seed—in other words, by making your start. What is the first thing you would do if you KNEW you would get your desire? What is the first step you would take in its accomplishment? TAKE IT! Do something to start, no matter on how small a scale. To begin, you know, is to be half done. Make the accomplishment of that desire the *sine qua non* of your existence, give to it all the thought and energy and riches you have to bring it into being, leave all other considerations in second place until you have won what you want.

That is the way great fortunes are made. That is the way miracles are performed. That is the only way you can put life into the nucleus of your desires and start them whirling and drawing to you whatever things you need for their manifestation.

Conditions, obstacles—they don't matter. Disclaim them, disregard them, and lay claim to the thing you want regardless of conditions. Like the seed in rocky soil, they may force your nucleus to work harder, to whirl faster, but give it vitality enough, and it will draw what it needs from the ends of the earth!

So don't work on poverty. Don't work on debts. That will merely bring more of these undesirables to you. Work on your idea, work on your nucleus—*believe that you receive*— and you will speedily draw to you all the riches you need to fill out the vacuums now caused by poverty and debts.

You have seen shoots of trees spring up on rocky ledges where there was scarcely enough nourishment to keep a bit of moss alive. And you have known such shoots to grow into mighty trees. How do they do it?

The seed of a tree is a nucleus. Plant it, and the first thing it does after it heats and germinates is to burst its shell and send forth a shoot—*upward*—using for that purpose the energy latent in the seed itself. In other words, it reaches out first to express life. It uses all the power it has to bring forth fruit. When it finds it has not enough energy in itself to accomplish this, it puts forth roots to draw the necessary elements from the soil about.

But if it happens to have fallen on a rocky ledge, it soon finds there is not enough soil to give it moisture or nourishment. Does it then despair? Not a bit of it! It sends its roots into every tiny crevice until they reach moisture and nourishment. It actually splits giant rocks asunder in its search for nutriment. It burrows through or around any obstacle until it exhausts the last flicker of life in itself or gets what it wants. Wherever they are, whatsoever may stand between, the shoot of the tree sends its roots seeking every element it needs for its growth and fruition.

First the stalk—then the roots. First the need—then the means to satisfy that need. First the nucleus—then the elements needed for its growth. The seed is a primary cause. The need, the nucleus, both are primary causes. Conditions—they are secondary. Given enough life in the nucleus, it will draw to itself the necessary means for growth regardless of conditions. The life in the seed is what counts—not the place where it falls.

All through Nature, you will find that same law. First the need, then the means. Use what you have to provide the vacuum, then draw upon the necessary elements to fill it. Reach up with your stalk, spread out your branches, provide the "pull" and you can leave to your roots the search for the necessary nourishment. If you have reached high enough, if you have made your magnet strong enough, you can draw to yourself whatever elements you need, no matter if they be at the ends of the earth!

God formed a Seed of Life which is you. He gave it power to attract to itself everything it needs for its growth, just as He did with the seed of the tree. He gave it power to draw to itself everything it needs for the fruition of its DESIRES, just as He did with the tree. But He did even more for you. He gave your Seed of Life power to attract to itself everything it needs for its *infinite expression!* He asks of you only that you make your desires strong enough, your faith in their drawing power great enough, to attract to you anything necessary to their fruition.

You see, Life is intelligent. Life is all-powerful. And Life is always and everywhere seeking expression. What is more, it is never satisfied. It is constantly seeking greater and fuller expression. The moment a tree stops growing, that moment the life in it starts seeking elsewhere for means to better express itself. The moment you stop expressing more and more of Life, that moment Life starts looking around for other and better outlets.

The only thing that can restrict Life is the channel through which it works. The only limitation upon it is the limitation you put upon it.

Over in Japan, they have taken the shoots of oak trees, and by binding a wire tightly around the main root at the point where the trunk begins, they have stunted the growth to such an extent that instead of great oaks eighty or a hundred feet high, these shoots reproduce all their qualities in dwarfed trees twelve or fourteen inches in height! These stunted trees live as long as regular trees, but they express only the millionth part of the life an oak should manifest.

We look upon that as abnormal, and so it is, yet it is being done all around us every day. Men bind their subconscious minds with wires of fear and worry. They put clamps of limitation upon their channels of supply. Then they wonder why they don't express more life in their bodies, why more of happiness and comfort is not evidenced in their surroundings.

God put a seed of Himself into you. That seed He called DESIRE. He gave it infinite power to draw to itself whatever it needs for expression. But He gave you free will—in other words, He left it with you to direct that expression— to draw upon it to the full or to put clamps upon it, as you like.

There lies in you the aegis of a Napoleon, a Lincoln, an Edison—anything you wish. All that is necessary is to stir up the Seed of God in you, and give it channels for expression. You can be what you want to be, if you want it strongly enough, if you believe in it firmly enough to make it your dominant desire.

How did Annette Kellerman, from a hopelessly crippled child, become one of the world's most perfectly formed women? By stirring up the Seed of Life in her limbs, through her earnest DESIRE for strength and beauty, by giving them work to do, ways in which to express life! How did George Jowett, from a cripple at eleven, become the world's strong man at twenty-one? By stirring up the Seed of Life in him through his overmastering DESIRE to be strong—by giving his muscles first a little, then more and more of work to do.

How did Reza Khan, from an ordinary trooper in the Persian army, rise to the rulership of Persia? How did a water boy win the throne of Afghanistan?

One and all, they stirred up the Seed of Life in them through DESIRE and Faith. One and all, they reached up and out, using freely all the power they had in the serene confidence that there was plenty more behind. Obstacles? They knew that obstacles were merely negative conditions that would disappear as darkness disappears when you turn on the light. It was the *prize* they kept their eyes upon. And it was the *prize* that they reached out for and plucked!

A few years ago, if anyone had told the neighbors of these men that today they would be rulers, he would have been laughed at as crazy. "Why, just look at their position," he would have been told. "Look at their circumstances, their surroundings. Look at the condition of the country. Consider their lack of training, of experience."

Conditions—all of them. Secondary causes. And these men had the vision to see beyond them—to go back to the *primary cause*—the Seed of God in themselves. They opened new channels for it to express itself. They reached up their stalks and spread out their branches and the Seed of Life in them drew to itself every element needed to bring forth their fruit.

At the heart of you is a seed—the Seed of God, the Seed of Life. In it is a perfect body, just as in every acorn there is a perfect oak. Not only that, but there is the power in it to draw to you every element you need to manifest a perfect body.

What do you care if circumstances have conspired to make you sick, or crippled or weak or infirm or ugly or old? If you are, it is because you or those around you have put the clamps of your fears or wrong beliefs upon the Seed of Life in you, and certain of your organs are stunted or dying.

The remedy? It is simple. Remove the clamps! Disregard your infirmity? It is only a condition—a LACK of Life. Then stir up the Seed of Life in you. Stir it up and charge it to draw to itself every element necessary to fill out the perfect image of your body that is in the seed.

Impossible? Have you ever heard of anything that is impossible to God? It is a Seed of God that is in you, and there is NOTHING of good it cannot draw to you!

The Law is—Use what you have, and more will be given you.

> *Let me not ask how difficult may be*
> *The work assigned to me.*
> *This only do I ask:*
> *Is this my task?*
>
> *Let me not ask if I be strong enough,*
> *Or if the road be rough.*
> *I only ask today,*
> *Is this the way?*
>
> —CLAUDE WEIMER

"Every good tree bringeth forth good fruit," said Jesus. "But a corrupt tree bringeth forth evil fruit. Every tree that bringeth not forth good fruit is hewn down and cast into the fire. Wherefore by their fruits ye shall know them."

What did Jesus mean by "Bearing fruit"? Didn't He have in mind methods of expressing the Seed of Life in you, making opportunities for it to expand and reach out to all those you come in contact with, doing something that makes this world a better place to live in?

And how does a tree go about the bearing of fruit? It brings forth a fragrant blossom first, does it not? When the blossom goes, it leaves the pistil, which gradually ripens into the luscious fruit.

The blossom is any idea of service, any means for making life more comfortable or enjoyable for those you live or deal with. The pistil is the action of turning that blossom into the beginning of the fruit by taking the first step to start the service, no matter how small that step may be. The luscious fruit is the finished service.

"That's fine!" I can hear many say, "I have the blossom— oh, a most fragrant blossom—but no means for turning it into the pistil or the fruit."

What does the branch have with which to start fruit? Enough nourishment for a start, but nothing over. Do you see the branch worrying on that account? Not a bit of it! It uses cheerfully everything it has, serene in the knowledge that providing more is the vine's problem. The branch has only to supply the *need*. The more it finds use for, the more it gets. Another branch may be just as big, but if the first one bears twice as much fruit, it will get twice as much nourishment, for the vine apportions its life-giving forces—not by size, but by needs. Wasn't it Jesus who said—"I am the vine, ye are the branches." Can you draw on Him for more than He can provide?

"Straight from a mighty bow this truth is driven: They fail, and they alone, who have not striven." They have a proverb in the East that a road of a thousand miles begins with a single step. Goethe expressed the thought when he wrote—

> *Are you in earnest? Seize this very minute;*
> *What you can do, or dream you can, BEGIN it!*
> *Boldness has genius, power and magic in it.*
> *Only engage, and then the mind grows heated;*
> *BEGIN, and then the work will be completed.*

"If ye abide in me," promised the Master, "and my words abide in you, ye shall *ask what ye will,* and it shall be done unto you. For herein is my Father glorified, that ye bear much fruit."

If you stir up the Seed of Life in you by strong DESIRES, if you provide it channels through which to express itself by taking the first step towards the accomplishment of those desires, you can ask for any element you need, and it will be given you.

But if you lose this day loitering, it will be the same story tomorrow and the day after. That which you are today is the fulfillment of yesterday's aspirations; that which you are tomorrow will be the achievement of today's vision. You can't stand still. You must go forward—or backward. Eternal progress is the Law of Being. If you meet its call, you will never fail to go on and on to greater and greater heights. As Florence Taylor so aptly put it—

> *Success is the sum of small efforts,*
> *Repeated day in and day out,*
> *With never a thought of frustration,*
> *With never a moment of doubt.*
> *Whatever your cherished ambition,*
> *Begin now to make it come true,*
> *Through efforts, repeated, untiring,*
> *Plus faith in the thing that you do.*

Health, riches, love—they are all *means* to an end, they are all conditions. The Seed of Life in you is the only thing that counts—that, and the channels you give it for expression. There is your PRIMARY CAUSE—all else is secondary. So disregard all else, and keep going back to it.

Do you want love? The mere desire is a proof of the availability of the love you want, for someone has rightly defined desire as God tapping at your door with His infinite supply. So plant the seeds of love by giving it to all you come in contact with. Plant the seeds freely, serenely, believingly, and the harvest is as sure as when you plant seeds of wheat in fertile ground.

Make it a practice to appreciate things and people. Use it all through the day whenever anything occurs that pleases you. Say silently, if you cannot do so audibly, "I appreciate you." And never miss an opportunity to say a kindly word of praise or thanks to those around you. As Amy Bower puts it—

> *We never know*
> *How far kind words may go.*
> *There is no way to measure*
> *Friendly smiles. They carry treasures*
> *Of courage, faith and love of man.*
> *And we may watch them grow*
> *Until their warmth*

*Infolds a multitude; returns to bless
The giver too with bread of happiness.*

A good affirmation to use is—"I so love that I see all good and give all good, and all good comes back to me."

Do you want riches? Wealth is largely a matter of consciousness. Many persons who want money, and who are striving for money, actually tend toward driving it away from them by reason of their tenseness of thought and their failure to realize the "money consciousness." In order to handle millions, one must learn to think in the terms and ideas of millions. Harriman once expressed this pregnant truth when he said: "It is just as easy to think and to talk in millions as in single dollars." This wizard of finance, whose feats were regarded by the public as closely approaching those of legerdemain, made this adage one of his cardinal principles of thought and action. He "thought and talked in millions," and his thought took form in action—his mental states took on material form—his ideals became realities.

There are many men in this country—in every city in this country—who have within them the germ-powers which, if allowed to develop and grow, would cause these men to become second Harrimans, or second Morgans, or even second Rockefellers. But practically none of these persons ever will really develop into this stage; in fact, the probability is that they will evolve merely into successful small shopkeepers, small news-stand keepers, or even small peanut-stand men—successful, in each case, but always on a small scale. They are content to think in single dollars—even in dimes— instead of thinking in millions. They manifest realities in the direct ratio of their ideals. Their thought takes form in actions of like calibre. Their mental states are reproduced in material form, but they are the same size in both subjective pattern and objective form.

*Just where thou art, shine forth and glow;
Just where thou art, 'tis better so;
Serve thou the Lord with perfect heart,
Not somewhere else, but where thou art.*

Emerson had a saying that you could travel the world over in search of beauty, but unless you had it within yourself, you would never find it, and the same is true of every good thing of life. The first step to success lies right where you are and in what you are doing. Until you have learned the lesson your present work holds for you, until you have learned to do it joyfully, lovingly, as to the Lord, you have not taken that first step towards the goal of your ambitions. You have not really begun.

Supply is an active force. It goes only to those who are alive, who are providing so many and such powerful magnets for it that they can "pull" it to themselves regardless of what obstacles may come between.

But suppose it is health you want? Suppose you are crippled or blind or bed-ridden. What then?

Why, then your remedy lies in breaking up the congealed life in your afflicted organ, and pouring it anew into the perfect mold.

And the way to break it up is by giving all you have of life to that one desire, by working up so intense a FEELING that it shall presently burst its shell and draw to it every element it needs for its perfect expression.

You can't do that by dabbling in mental work, the while you are depending partly upon drugs, partly upon other means. You must FEEL so strongly that your salvation lies in the Seed of God within you, you must BELIEVE so utterly in its power, that you are willing to sink or swim by it alone. Like Grant, you must have the grim determination to "fight it out along those lines, if it takes all summer!"

But it will not take "all summer." Once you get the spirit of it, you will find it by far the speediest and surest method there is. Often your relief will be immediate.

A writer in "Unity" tells of a friend who was suffering from a physical inharmony that threatened to become malignant, when all at once the thought came to her—"If God can't heal me, what can *this* do?" "This" referred to the drugs she was taking. Immediately she applied a cleansing substance to the troublous part, threw away the drugs and from that day had no further trouble.

In THE FORUM, recently, Winifred Rhoades told of an amusing happening in India, It seems that a pack animal slipped at a ferry in India some years ago, and a case of medicines was spilled. The colored pills were picked up and returned to their appropriate bottles, but with the 'white pills it was impossible to tell one kind from another. However, a young native gathered them up, and in spite of the missionary doctor's warning of the danger of using them ignorantly, he promptly made them the foundation of a widespread reputation.

When the missionary next appeared in that region, the young native greeted him with joy. "I owe all my prosperity to you!" he exclaimed. It seems that the bottle containing the assorted white pills he had picked up was the favorite in his shop. Patients came from far and near to get them. And in answer to the horrified doctor's question as to how he could administer them if he didn't know what they were meant for, he announced that he gave them to patients only when he didn't know what was the matter with them.

Dr. Richard C. Cabot of Harvard told a gathering of his fellow-medicos—"The body has a super wisdom and force which are biased in favor of life rather than death. What is this force? It is God, the healing power which supplies 90 percent of recovery." And on another occasion, he said—"If nature, assisted by the proper mental and emotional moods, is capable of curing an ulcer in three or four weeks, why isn't it possible for the same force to heal the same ulcer in three or four minutes, when the curative processes have been speeded up abnormally by the subject's passing through an intense religious (*emotional*) experience?" In "Man, the Unknown," Dr. Alexis Carrel told of having actually seen a cancerous growth on a man's hand cured in a few minutes.

You see, underneath all its seeming hardness, life is really a kindly force. Life is love. It is supply. It is health. It has in it every element we need to satisfy any right desire. So there is no need to look to this man, or that drug, or some outside agency, for the things you need. Go to the Primary Cause. Go to Life. Go to God!

"There is a time in every man's education," said Emerson, "when he arrives at the conviction that he must take *himself* for better or for worse *as his portion;* that though the wide universe is full of good, no kernel of nourishing corn can come to him but through his toil on that plot of ground given to him to till.

"The power which resides in him is new in nature, and none but he knows what he can do. *Nor does he know until he has tried.*"

> "*You are sick,*" *they said,* "*But that isn't the truth*"—
> *And the woman shook her head.*
> "*The Bible declares, he that dwelleth in God*
> *Shall not say, I am sick,*" *she said.*
> *And she held to the truth through a starless night,*
> *Till morning proved that her words were right.*
>
> "*You are tired,*" *they said. But she smiled at that.*
> "*How can I be tired,*" *said she,*
> "*When the only work is work for God,*
> *And He is my life, you see?*"
> *And she quietly went her busy way,*
> *With a happy song in her heart all day.*

> "You are poor," they said. But she only thought,
> "How little they know! God speed
> The day when the world awakes to find
> That love is its only need."
> And she still maintained, as her fortune grew,
> Not money but love—if they only knew!
>
> For the world knows not of the peace that comes
> To a soul at one with God.
> It is only those who are toiling on
> In the path the Master trod
> Who can feel, through the dark, that loving hand,
> And holding it fast, can understand.

What was it that made Napoleon Master of most of Europe? Not native genius. Not brilliant intellect. In his class at the Military Academy, he stood forty-sixth—and there were only sixty-five in the class!

The genius that made Napoleon was first his intense DESIRE for power, and then *his colossal belief in his own destiny!* He had no fear in battle, because he believed the bullet was not made that could kill him. He had no hesitation in attempting the seemingly impossible, because he believed the very stars in their courses would stoop to sweep the obstacles from his path.

You see, the secret of success lies in this: There is inside you a Seed of Life capable of drawing to you any element you need, to bring to fruition whatever of good you desire. But like all other seeds, its shell must be broken before the kernel inside can use its attractive power. And that shell is thicker, harder, than the shell of any seed on earth. Only one thing will break it—heat from WITHIN—a *desire* so strong, a determination so intense, that you cheerfully throw everything you have into the scale to win what you want. Not merely your work and your money and your thought, but the willingness to stand or fall by the result—to do or to die. Like the Master when He cursed the fig tree for its barrenness, you are willing to demand of the Seed of Life in you that it *bear fruit or perish.*

That is the secret of every great success. That is the means by which all of life, from the beginning of time, has won what it needed.

What was it gave to certain animals protective shells, to others speed, to still others a sting, to those who needed them claws or horns? What gave to the bold and strong the means to destroy, to the weak and cowardly facilities for hiding or escape? What but the Seed of Life in each, giving to every form of life the means that form craved to preserve its skin.

Always the seed in each form of life responded to the call of that life—*"Give me so-and-so or I perish."*

Since the very creation of the earth, Life has been threatened by every kind of danger. Had it not been stronger than any other power in the Universe—were it not indeed a part of God Himself—it would have perished ages ago. But God who gave it to us endowed it with unlimited resource, unlimited energy. No other force can defeat it. No obstacle can hold it back.

What is it that saves men in dire extremity, who have exhausted every human resource and finally turned to God in their need? What but the unquenchable flame of God in them—the Seed of Life He has given to each of us—with power to draw to us whatever element we feel that we need to save us from extinction.

What do business leaders advise young people today? Live within your income? No, indeed! Go *into debt!* Reach out! Spread yourself! Then dig the harder to catch up!

You are entitled to just as much of the good things of life as Ford or Rockefeller or Morgan, or any of the rich men around you. But it is not THEY who owe it to you. And it is not the world that owes you a living. The world and they owe you nothing but honest pay for the exact service you render them.

The one who owes you everything of good—riches and honor and happiness—is the Seed of Life inside you. Go to it! Stir it up! Don't rail against the world. You get from it what you put into it—nothing more. Wake up the Seed of God inside you! Demand of it that it bring you the elements you need for riches or success. Demand—and make your need seem as urgent as must have been the need of the crustacean to develop a shell, of the bird to grow wings, of the bear to give it fur.

Demand—and KNOW THAT YOU RECEIVE! The Seed of Life in you is just as strong as ever it was in those primitive animals of pre-historic days. If it could draw from the elements whatever means it required to enable them to survive, don't you suppose it can do the same today to provide you with the factors you consider essential to your well-being?

True, these factors are different from those called for in primitive times, but do you suppose that matters to the Seed of Life? Everything in this world is made up of energy. Don't you suppose it is as easy to pour that energy into one mold as into another?

Many seem to think that riches and success are a matter of luck. They are not luck. They are a matter of DEMANDING MUCH from the Seed of God inside you, and then insisting upon those demands being met.

The trouble with most people is that they are looking to some force outside themselves to bring them riches or happiness. The superstitious carry a rabbit's foot or an amulet, believing it will bring them luck. The religious carry medals or images or the relic of some Saint. It never occurs to them that they have the means of going direct to God. God seems too impalpable, too shadowy and far away. His apparent isolation, His seeming detachment from their work-a-day world, makes Him appear too unsubstantial to depend upon in real need. They want something they can see and feel and talk to. Something with a substance like their own. Hence the demand for statues and pictures and shrines and relics Hence, too, the need for Saints and Priests—intercessors, nearer to the Great One than ordinary mortals can hope to reach.

But direct contact is always better than even the most potent intermediary. And you HAVE the direct contact, any time you want to use it.

You are a Tree of Life. The seed of you is a Seed of God—part of Him as much as the acorn is part of the oak. And that Seed has all the properties of God, just as the acorn has all the potential properties of the oak. It can draw to you every element you need to make yours the most perfect tree in the garden, the most fruitful.

So, instead of depending upon the stars, or a rabbit's foot, or an amulet, or even the Saints, put your faith in the Seed of God, which is the animating part of you. No matter what your circumstances may be, no matter what obstacles may conspire to hold you down, look—NOT merely to the means at hand, NOT to circumstances or conditions— but to that never-failing power of the Seed inside you to draw to you any element you believe you MUST have to survive.

That is the way to make your "Star," your "Destiny," work for you. Only the "Star," the "Destiny," is right inside YOU. It is the Seed of God, the Seed of Life in YOU which your desire, your faith and your need have started into action. It is stronger than any circumstances. It can overcome any condition. So bless it and baptize it, *and stir it up!*

Bless it morning and evening, but when the urgent need arises—DEMAND! Demand that it bestir itself. Demand that it draw to you whatever elements you need. Demand— and *give all* as you demand all—make it a matter of life or death, survive or perish.

The Magic Word

There is a point in the tree, you know, below which the "pull" of the leaves has little power. That is the point to which the roots must deliver the water, or the tree will never flower or bear fruit.

There is a point in your circumstances or your business at which the pull of your Seed of Life does not make itself felt. That is the point to which your efforts must deliver the fruit of your work, or your desire will die still-born.

So when you demand, first GIVE—throw every bit of effort you have into reaching the point at which the Seed of Life will take over the work. Give all that you can to the work in hand, and don't forget to give to the Lord as well. It is this which makes so successful the prayers of those who, demanding riches, throw all their scanty store into the plate, and depend solely upon that Seed of God in them to supply their needs. When you can do this, believing, the world is yours.

> *When things go wrong, as they sometimes will,*
> *When the road you're trudging seems all up hill,*
> *When the funds are low and the debts are high,*
> *And you want to smile, but you have to sigh,*
> *When care is pressing you down a bit,*
> *REST—if you must—but don't you quit.*
>
> *Success is failure turned inside out—*
> *The silver tint of the cloud of doubt,*
> *And you never can tell how close you are,*
> *It may be near when it seems afar.*
> *So stick to the fight when you're hardest hit—*
> *It's when things seem worse that you mustn't quit.*

EXERCISE FOR CHAPTER SIXTEEN

All things therefore whatsoever ye would that men should do unto you, even so do ye also unto them; for this is the law and the prophets.

Someone in Omaha studied that Golden Rule, and out of it found the solution to much of Nebraska's jobless problem in the last big depression. He brought together a number of jobless men and women, and started them doing things to help others!

Forgetting their own troubles, they looked about them for ways to help others more unhappy and unfortunate than themselves and organized the All Omaha Self Help Society. They do farming, craft work and canning. They build houses, repair them, tend yards, do housework, care for children, and perform any service that offers which is of value to the community. Where money is available, they accept pay for their services and turn it into wheat and flour and fuel and shelter. They have improved their condition and that of all around them, without waiting for business to pick up or for some government agency to give them a lift. And in scores of parts of the country, similar groups have done the same.

In times of quandary, when you seem at the end of your rope, if you will only stop and think awhile, you will nearly always find that you have the BEGINNINGS of the solution of your problem in your mind, or somewhere ready to your hand. Use that beginning to start—no matter on how small a scale.

Alice Foote MacDougall built a business that, before the depression of the '30's, was worth $5,000,000. Yet she started with a little booth in Grand Central Station where she sold coffee. One blustery winter's day, everyone that came in seemed so cold and hungry that she sent home for her waffle iron and the necessary ingredients, and served waffles free to all who came for coffee. Those free waffles made her famous. They were the start that built for her a string of restaurants and a good-sized fortune.

The stories of that kind we might tell are legion. There was the poor farmer's wife who gave some of the strawberry preserves she was making to a youngster from High School who had stopped by for a drink. He thought them so good that he asked if he couldn't sell some of them to neighbors. From that start she built a profitable business.

The famous Jones Farm Sausage got its start from the talk of neighbors and friends who had tasted this delicious sausage at the Jones' table. And many another successful business has started on as small a scale.

The great thing is the start—to see an opportunity for service, and to start doing it, even though in the beginning you serve but a single customer—and him for nothing.

> *In life's small things be resolute and great*
> *To keep thy muscles trained.*
> *Knowst thou when Fate thy measure takes?*
> *Or when she'll say to thee*
> *"I find thee worthy, do this thing for me!"*

STRONG DESIRE ESSENTIAL TO SUCCESS

I

Desire Power is one of the many phases of Personal Power—of that Personal Power which flows into and through the individual from that great source of the All-Power of All-Things which in this instruction is know as POWER.

You do not create your own Personal Power of any kind, though you may modify it, adapt it, develop it, and direct it. POWER, the source of All-Power, has always existed and will always exist. You generate Personal Power by drawing upon the great Source and Fount of All-Power; by opening your natural channels to its inflow; and by supplying it with the proper physical and mental mechanism by means of which it is enabled to express and manifest itself efficiently.

An old writer once said: "Few speakers succeed who attempt merely to make people think—they want to be made to feel. People will pay liberally to be made to feel or to laugh, while they will begrudge a sixpence for instruction or talk that will make them think. The reasons are palpable and plain: it is heart against head; soul against logic; and soul is bound to win every time." Cardinal Newman once said: "The heart is commonly reached, not through reason, but through the imagination, by means of direct impressions, by descriptions. Persons influence us, voices melt us, deeds inflame us."

One has but to recall instances of the great influence exerted over the public mind by the emotional appeals to affection or dislike, to prejudices for or against, to desires, ambitions, aspirations, cravings, longings and things eagerly "wanted," made by orators, politicians, statesmen, actors and preachers, in order to realize the potent effect of Emotion, Affection and Desire upon men's thoughts, opinions, beliefs and convictions.

A modern writer says: "A large part of the business of life consists in moving the emotions and desires of men so as to get them to act." Another says: "The successful man is he who is able to persuade the crowd that he has something that they want, or that they want something that he has." The successful salesman, advertising man or any other man who has things to sell other men, all bring into play the force of Desire in those whom they are seeking to interest in their projects. They appeal to the "want" or "want to" side of the mind of men. They play upon men's sympathies, their prejudices, their hopes, their fears, their desires, their aversions.

Men "do things" and "act" because of the motive power of their emotional nature, particularly in the form of Affection and Desire. This is the only reason impelling or influencing men to "do things." Were this motive power absent, there would be no action or doing of things; there would be no reason or cause for such action or doing, in that event. We act and do solely because we "like" and "want." Were the emotional element absent, there would be no element of volition. Without Desire we would make no choices, would exercise no decision, would perform no actions. Without the "want" and "want to," there would be no "will to do," and no "doing." Desire is the motive power of Action; take away the motive power and there cannot be and will not be any movement, activity or volition. Without the motive power of Desire, the machinery of voluntary action ceases to operate, and comes to a complete standstill.

An old writer, whose words have been preserved for us though his name is unknown to the present writers, enunciates a profound truth in the following rather startling statement:

"Every deed that we do, good or bad, is prompted by Desire. We are charitable because we wish to relieve our inner distress at the sight of suffering; or from the urge of sympathy, with its desire to express its nature; or from the desire to be respected in this world, or to secure a comfortable place in the next one. One man is kind because he desires to be kind—because it gives him satisfaction and content to be kind. Another man is unkind because he desires to be so—because it gives him satisfaction and content to be so. One man does his duty because he desires to do it—he obtains a higher emotional satisfaction and content from duty well done than he would from neglecting it in accordance with some opposing desires. Another man yields to the desire to shirk his duty—he obtains greater satisfaction and content from refraining from performing his duty, in favor of doing other and contrary things which possess a greater emotional value to himself.

The religious man is religious in his actions, because his religious desires are stronger than are his irreligious ones—he finds a greater satisfaction and content in religious actions than in the pursuits of the worldly-minded. The moral man is moral because his moral desires are stronger than his immoral ones—he obtains a greater degree of emotional satisfaction and content in being moral than in being immoral. Everything we do is prompted by Desire in some shape or form, high or low. Man cannot be Desireless, and still act in one way or another—or in any way whatsoever. Desire is the motive-power behind all action—it is a natural law of Life. Everything from the atom to the monad; from the monad to the insect; from the insect to man; from Man to

Nature; and possibly from Nature to God; everything from lowest to highest and from highest to lowest— everything that is—is found to act and to do things, to manifest action and to perform work, by reason of the power and force of Desire. Desire is the animating power, the energizing force, and the motive-power in, under, and behind all natural processes, activities and events.

There is a general rule concerning Desire which it is important that you should note and remember. The rule is as follows: *"The degree of force, energy, will, determination, persistence and continuous application manifested by an individual in his aspirations, ambitions, aims, performances, actions and work is determined primarily by the degree of 'want' and 'want to' concerning that object."*
So true is this principle that some who have studied its effects have announced the aphorism: *"You can have or be anything that you want—if you only want it hard enough."* To "want a thing hard enough" is equivalent to "paying the price" for it—the price of the sacrifice of lesser desires and "wants"; the casting off of the non-essentials, and the concentration of Desire upon the one essential idea or thing, and the application of the will to its attainment or accomplishment.
Much that we have been in the habit of ascribing to the possession and the manifestation of a "strong will" has really been due to the element of Will which is called Conation, i.e., Desire tending toward expression in Will-action. The man filled with an ardent, fierce, burning, craving and urge for and toward a certain object, will call to his aid the latent powers of his Will, and of his Intellect—these under the motive power and stimulus of Desire will manifest unusual activity and energy toward the accomplishment of the desired end. Desire has well been called the Flame which produces the heat which generates the Steam of Will.
Very few persons, comparatively, know how to Desire with sufficient intensity and insistence. They content themselves with mere "wishing" and mild "wanting." They fail to experience that Insistent Desire, which is one of the important elements of the Master Formula of Attainment. They do not know what it is to feel and manifest that intense, eager, longing, craving, insistent demanding, ravenous Desire which is akin to the persistent, insistent, ardent, overwhelming desire of the drowning man for a breath of air; of the shipwrecked or desert-lost man for a drink of water; of the famished man for bread and meat; of the fierce, wild creature for its mate; of the mother for the welfare of her children. Yet, if the truth were known, the desire for success of the men who have accomplished great things has often been as great as these.

We are not necessarily slaves to our Desires; we may master the lower or disadvantageous desires by Will, under the Power of the "I AM I," or Master Self. We may transmute lower desires into higher, negatives into positives, hurtful into helpful, in this way. We may become Masters of Desire, instead of being mastered by it. But before we may do so, we must first desire to do so, to accomplish and to attain this end. We may even rise to the heights of Will—the place where the "I AM I" may say, truthfully, "I Will to Will" and "I Will to Desire"; but even there we must first desire to so "Will to Will" and "Will to Desire."

Even at these sublime heights of Egohood, we find Desire to be the fundamental and elemental Motive Power: this because it abides at the very heart of things—the heart of ourselves—the Heart of Life. Even there, we essay and accomplish the highest deeds and acts of Will solely and simply because they serve to "content our spirit," to give us the highest degree of "self satisfaction"—to gratify, satisfy and give expression and manifestation to our greatest, most insistent, most persistent and strongest "want" and "want to."

MAGNETIC POWER OF DESIRE

The strongest and most persistent desires of the individual tend to attract to him (or him to) that which is closely related to or correlated with those desires," That is to say: the strong insistent desires of a person tend to attract to him those things which are closely related to such desires; and, at the same time, tend to attract him toward those related things. The Attractive Desire of Desire operates in two general ways, viz., (1) to attract to the individual the things closely related to his desires; and (2) to attract the individual to such related things.

In your own experience, in all probability, you have experienced many cases of the operation of this subtle law of Nature. You have become intensely interested in some particular subject, and your desire for further progress and attainment along the lines of that subject has been actively aroused. Then you have noticed the strange and peculiar way in which persons and things related to that subject have come under your observation and attention—sometimes even being apparently forced upon you apart from any act on your part. In the same way, you have found yourself attracted in certain directions in which, unknown to you, were to be found persons or things related to the subject of your desire, information concerning that subject, conditions in which the subject was involved or being manifested. In short, you have found that things happened "as if" you were either attracting persons, things and circumstances to you, or else that you were being attracted, drawn or "led" to such persons, things or circumstances.

Under such conditions, you will find arising on all sides certain events connected with and related to the subject of your desire; books containing information concerning it; persons having some connection with it; conditions in which that subject plays an important part. You will find, on the one hand, that you seem to have become a center of attraction for things, persons and circumstances related to that subject; or, on the other hand, that you are being attracted to certain centers of attraction related to that subject. In short, you will discover that you have set into operation certain subtle forces and principles which have "correlated" you with all related to that subject.

More than this, you will find that if you will maintain for a considerable time a continuous and persistent interest and desire in that particular subject, you will have established a vortex-center of attraction for that which is related to the subject. You will have set into operation a mental whirlpool, steadily spreading its circumference of influence, which draws into itself and to your central point the related and correlated things, persons and circumstances.

This is one of the reasons why after you "get things going" in any particular line of interest and desire, things tend to "come easier" to and for you as time passes. In such cases, that which required enormous effort in the earlier stages seems to move almost automatically in the later ones. These are matters of common and almost universal experience with those who have been actively engaged in any particular line of work in which strong interest and insistent desire have been aroused and maintained.

So, you see, Desire Power tends not only to develop and evolve within you the qualities and powers necessary to enable you to manifest and express yourself along the lines of the desires persistently held by you; it also tends to attract to you, and you to them, the things, persons, circumstances and conditions related to or correlated with the subject of such desires. In other words, Desire Power employs every means at its disposal in order to express and manifest itself more fully, and (through you) to attain its object and end—its greatest possible degree of satisfaction and realization. When you have thoroughly aroused Desire Power within you, and have created for it a strong, positive focal center of influence, you have set into operation powerful forces of Nature, operating along subconscious and invisible lines of activity. In this connection, remember the adage: *"You may have anything you want—if you only want it hard enough."*

The attractive force of Desire Power operates in many different ways. In addition to the "drawing power" operating along the lines of "something like telepathy" of which we have spoken, it also operates in other ways on the subconscious planes of the mind in order to influence, guide and direct the person to the other persons, things, conditions and circumstances related or correlated to or with the particular desire which is being persistently and insistently held by that person. Under its influence, the subconscious mentality raises to the levels of consciousness new ideas, thoughts, plans, which if applied will tend to "lead" the person in the direction of the things which will serve to aid him in the realization of those desires which he is insistently harboring.

In this way, the person is led to the related things, just as in the other ways the things are led to him. Desire Power pushes, as truly as it pulls—it urges you forward as truly as it attracts things to you. In some cases the process is entirely subconscious, and the person is amazed when he finds "by chance" (!) that he has "stumbled upon" helpful things in places in which he had least expected to find them, and in places to which he had apparently been led by Chance. But there is no Chance about it; persons are undoubtedly "led to" helpful things and conditions, but by Desire Power operating along the lines of the subconscious mentality, and not by Chance.

Many successful men could tell how often in their respective careers, at critical times, the most peculiar happenings have been experienced by them, seemingly "by chance" or "by accident,' which served as the means of transforming defeat into victory. In this way they acquired "by chance" some important bit of information serving to supply the missing link in their mental chain, or else giving them a clue to that which had previously escaped their thought. Or, perhaps, they unexpectedly "ran into" the person who afterward turned out to be the one particular person who alone could have helped them in certain ways. Or, again, they have picked up at random the particular newspaper, magazine or book which either gave them the required information, or else mentioned some other book or thing which filled the need.

These things happen so often, and in such a striking way, that many men of active experience have learned to expect them, to rely upon them, and to act upon them. Not knowing the true underlying causes of the happenings, they usually refrain from mentioning their experiences to their friends for fear of being regarded as superstitious or credulous; but if the subject happens to be introduced in confidential conversation between men of this kind, it will be found that the instances cited are numerous, and are so strikingly similar in general nature that the careful thinker is forced to the conclusion that there is some fundamental principle involved in the events, and that there is a logical sequence of cause and effect indicated.

Not knowing the true cause of these happenings, men are prone to ascribe them to "luck," fate, destiny, chance or else to think of them simply as "one of those things beyond explanation." Some men who have become familiar with them have learned to recognize them readily when they experience them, by reason of a "feeling" that "here is another of those things." They learn to distinguish between a mere general and vague notion, and a "sure enough hunch." Sometimes, men think that these things are the result of the aid of a kindly Providence operating in their behalf; others feel that they have helpers "on the other side"; still others feel that there is "something almost uncanny" about the whole thing; but so long as it is perceived to operate in their behalf all are willing to take advantage of the aid of the Unknown Power.

Of course, the subconscious mentality of the individual is the "helper," or "directing genius" in such cases, and the happenings are merely phases of the general phenomena of the Subconscious. But, nevertheless, Desire Power is the animating principle involved. The subconscious mentality, like the conscious mentality, is energized and aroused into activity by the urge of

Desire Power. Desire Power employs every possible form of energy, activity and motive-power at its command; and also presses into service all kinds of machinery and instruments, mental and physical. The Fire of Desire kindles every faculty of the mind, on conscious and subconscious planes, and sets them all into active work on its behalf. Without Desire Power in some form or phase, none of these faculties would manifest activity; where activity is manifested by them, there is always implied the presence and urge of Desire Power.

Sometimes Desire Power will operate in strangely indirect ways in order to accomplish its results. By means of the "under the surface" perception of the subconscious faculties, Desire Power seemingly perceives that "the longest way 'round is the quickest way home," and it proceeds to cause the individual to pursue that "longest way 'round" in order to attain his desire in the shortest possible time. In such cases it often acts so as to upset and overturn the plans which one has carefully mapped out; the result makes it seem to one that failure and defeat, instead of victory and success, have come to him. It will sometimes tear the person away from his present comparatively satisfactory environment and conditions, and then lead him over rock roads and hard trails; and finally, when he has almost despaired of attaining success, he finds it literally thrust upon him.

Such instances are not invariable, of course, but they occur sufficiently often and with such characteristically marked features that they must be recognized. It often happens that, as one who has experienced it has said, "It seems as if one were grabbed by the back of his neck, lifted out of his set environment and occupation, dragged roughly over a painful road, and then thrust forcibly but kindly upon the throne of success or at least into the throne room with the throne in plain sight before him."

But, at the last, those who have experienced these strenuous activities of Desire Power operating through the subconscious nature and in many other ways are found to agree universally in the statement, "The end justified the means; the thing is worth the price paid for it." It requires philosophy and faith to sustain one when he is undergoing experiences of this kind, but the knowledge of the law and principle in operation will of course greatly aid him. The right spirit to maintain in such cases is that expressed in the phrase, "It's a great life, if you don't weaken."

Desire Power employs freely the subconscious faculties in its work of Realization through Attraction. It employs these in man just as it employs them in the case of the homing pigeon, the migrating birds, the bee far from its hive—it supplies the "homing instinct" to the man seeking success, as well as to the animal seeking refuge. It is said that animals separated from their mates, seemingly are attracted to them over long distances. Lost animals find their way home, though many miles over strange country have to be traveled. Let a person establish a "refuge" for birds, and the birds will soon begin to travel toward it—even strange species from long distances putting in an appearance. Water fowls travel unerringly toward water; the roots of trees manifest the same sense of direction toward water and rich soil.

In high and low, the Law of Desire Attraction manifests its power. Man is under the law, and may even cause the law to work for him when he understands its nature. Man may harness Desire Power just as he has harnessed other great forces of Nature—may harness it and set it to work for him. Once set to work for him, this power will work "without haste, and without rest" toward the end impressed upon it— it will work for him while he is awake and working otherwise, and when he is asleep and resting from his conscious work. Desire is the "force of forces," because it is the inmost kernel of all the other forms of natural force, physical or mental. All force depends upon inner Attraction or Repulsion—and these are but the manifestation of Desire Power, positive or negative.

THE MASTER FORMULA FOR GETTING WHAT YOU WANT

The Master Formula of Attainment, stated in popular form, is as follows:

"You may have anything you want, provided that you (1) know exactly what you want, (2) want it hard enough, (3) confidently expect to attain it, (4) persistently determine to obtain it, and (5) are willing to pay the price of its attainment."

We shall now ask you to consider three of the above five elements of the Master Formula of Attainment, viz., the element of Definite Ideals, or "knowing exactly what you want"; the element of Insistent Desire, or "wanting it hard enough"; the element of Balanced Compensation, or "being willing to pay the price of its attainment." Each of these three elements is highly important, and should be carefully examined and considered. Let us begin with the first requisite, i.e. "Knowing exactly what you want."

When you consider the question, "Exactly what do I want?" you will be apt to regard it as one quite easy to answer. But after you begin to consider the question in detail, and in real earnest, you will discover two very troublesome obstacles in your way on the road to the correct answer. The two obstacles are as follows: (1) the difficulty in ascertaining a clear and full idea of your desires, aspirations, ambitions, and hopes; and (2) the difficulty in ascertaining which ones of a number of conflicting desires, aspirations, ambitions, and hopes you "want" more than you do those opposing them.

You will find yourself with "the divine discontent" of a general dissatisfaction with your present condition, circumstances, possessions and limitations. You will feel, perhaps strongly, the "raw desire" of the elemental Desire Power within you, but you will not have clearly outlined in your mind the particular directions in which you wish that elemental force to proceed into manifestation and expression.

You will often feel that you wish that you were somewhere other than where you now are; that you were doing something different from what you are now doing; that you possessed things other and better than you now possess; or that your present limitations were removed, thus giving you a wider and fuller expression and manifestation of the power which you feel to be within you: all these general feelings will be experienced by you, but you will not be able to picture clearly to yourself just what "other things" you really want to take the place of those which are now your own.

Then, when you attempt to form the clear picture, and definite idea, of what you want, you will find you want *many* things, some of them opposing each other, each offering attractive features, each bidding actively for your favor and acceptance—thus rendering a choice and definite decision very difficult. You find yourself suffering from an embarrassment of riches. Like the perplexed lover in the song, you say, "How happy would I be with either, were t'other fair charmer away." Or, like the psychological donkey who was placed at an equidistant point between two equally tempting haystacks, and who died of hunger because he couldn't make up his mind which one he wanted most, you may remain inactive because of strong conflicting desire-motives.

It is because of one or both of the above-mentioned conditions that the great masses of persons do not avail themselves of the great elemental urge of Desire Power. It is there, ready to exert its power, but they lack definite direction and power of decision, and so remain, like the vegetables or the lower animals, content to allow Nature to work along the instinctive lines of self-protection, propagation, etc., without employing initiative or self-direction.

The few of the race who break these barriers, and who strike out for themselves, are found to have known very clearly "just what they wanted," and to have "wanted it hard," and to have been willing to pay the price of attainment. In order to set to work the forces of Desire Power in a special direction, the individual must make clear an ideal path over which they may travel, as well as to arouse the forces so as to cause them to travel over that path.

Self-Analysis. You will find that a scientific application of the principle of Self-Analysis, or mental stock-taking, will aid you materially in overcoming the two great obstacles in the Path of Attainment, which we have just mentioned. Self-Analysis in this case consists of a careful analysis of your elements of Desire, to the end that you may discover which of these elements are the strongest, and that you may clearly understand just what these strongest elements are really like in character. You are advised to "think with pencil and paper" in this work of self-analysis—it will greatly aid you in crystallizing your thought and, besides, will give a definite and logical form to the results of your work. The following suggestions and advice will aid you materially in this task.

Begin by asking yourself the question: *"What are my strongest desires? What do I 'want' and 'want to' over and above anything and everything else? What are my highest Desire-Values?"* Then proceed to "think with pencil and paper," and thus to answer your important question above stated.

Take your pencil and begin to write down your strongest desires—your leading "wants" and "want tos"—as they come into your consciousness in response to your inquiry. Write down carefully the things and objects, the aims and ideals, the aspirations and ambitions, the hopes and confident expectations, which present themselves for notation in the course of your mental stock-taking. Note all of them, without regard to the question of whether or not you ever expect to be able to secure or attain them.

Put them all down on the list, no matter how ridiculous and unattainable they may seem to you at the time. Do not allow yourself to be overcome by the magnificent aims and ideals, aspirations and ambitions, which thus present themselves. Their very existence in your Desire-nature is, in a measure, the prophecy of their own fulfillment. As Napoleon once said: "Nothing is too magnificent for a soldier of France!" You are that soldier of France! Do not impose limitations on your Desire-nature in this way. If a magnificent desire is within you, it should be respected—so put it down on the list.

By this process of Self-Analysis you bring to the surface of your consciousness all the various feelings, desires, longings and cravings which have been dwelling in your subconscious mind. Many of these deep desires are like sleeping giants—your exploration of your subconscious mental regions will arouse these—will cause them "to sit up and take notice," as it were. Do not be frightened by these awakening sleepers. Nothing that you find there is alien to you. Even though you may find it necessary to transmute them, or to inhibit them in favor of more advantageous desires, at a later stage of your work, do not now deny them a place on your list—put them down on paper. The list must be an honest one, therefore be honest with yourself in the analysis.

At first, you will find that your list is a more or less higgledy-piggledy conglomeration of "wants" and "want tos," apparently having but little or no logical order or systematic relation. Do not let this disturb you, however—all this will be taken care of as you proceed; order and arrangement will establish themselves almost automatically when the proper time arrives. The main thing at this stage is to get all of your stronger desires into the list. Be sure to exhaust your subconscious mind of strong desires—dig out of that mine anything and everything that has strength in it.

The next step is that of the cold-blooded, ruthless, elimination of the weakest desires, with the idea and purpose that in the end there will be a "survival of the fittest" on your list. Begin by running over your list, striking off the weaker and less insistent—the mere temporary and passing—desires, and those which you clearly recognize as likely to bring you but little if any permanent satisfaction, continued happiness and lasting content.

In this way you will create a new list of the stronger desires, and those having a greater permanent and satisfying value. Then, examining this list, you will find that some of the items will still stand out from the others by reason of their greater comparative strength and greater degree of permanent value. Make a new list of these successful candidates, including only those possessing the greatest strength and value to you, and dropping the others from the list. Then continue this process of elimination of the weakest and the least satisfying until you reach that point where you feel that any further elimination would result in cutting away live wood.

By this time you will have become aware of a most significant and important fact, namely, that as your list has grown smaller, the strength and value of the surviving desires have grown greater. As the old gold-miners expressed it, you are now "getting down to pay dirt"—getting down to the region in which the nuggets and rich ore abide. When you have reached this stage, you will do well to stop work for the time being; this will give you a needed mental rest, and will also furnish your subconscious mentality with the opportunity to do some work for you along its own particular lines.

When you again take up your list for consideration, you will find a new general order and arrangement of its items pictured in your mind. You will find that these remaining desires have grouped themselves into several general classes. Your subconscious mental faculties will have performed an important task for you. Then you will be ready to compare these general classes, one with the other, until you are able to select certain classes, which seem stronger than the others. Then you will be ready to proceed to the task of eliminating the weaker general classes, making a new list of the stronger ones.

After working along these general lines for a time, with intervals of rest and recuperation, and for subconscious digestion and elimination, you will find that you have before you a list composed of but a comparatively few general classes of "wants" and "want tos"—each of which possesses a far greater degree of strength and value than you had previously suspected. Your subconscious mind has been working its power upon these classes of desires, and they have evolved to a higher stage of strength, definiteness, clearness and power. You are beginning at last to find out "just what you want," and are also well started on your way to "wanting it hard enough."

General Rules of Selection. In your task of selection, elimination, "boiling down" and chopping away the dead wood, etc., you will do well to observe the three following general Rules of Selection:

I. *The Imperative Requisite.* In selecting your strongest desires for your list, you are not required to pay attention to any fears lurking in your mind that any of the particular desires are apparently unattainable—that they are beyond your power of achievement, and are rendered impossible by apparently unsurmountable obstacles. You are not concerned with such questions at this time and place—ignore them for the present. You are here concerned merely with the question of whether or not your "want" or "want to" concerning a certain thing is felt "hard enough" for you to sacrifice other desirable things—whether you feel that the particular desire is of sufficient value for you to "pay the price" of its attainment, even though that price be very high. Remember the old adage: "Said the gods to man, 'Take what thou wilt—but pay for it!' " If you are not willing to "pay the price," and to pay it in full, then you do not "want it hard enough" to render it one of your Prime Desires.

II. *The Test of Full Desire.* We have told you that, *"Desire has for its object something that will bring pleasure or get rid of pain, immediately or remote, for the individual or for some one in whom he is interested."* Therefore, in passing upon the comparative strength and value of your respective desires, or general classes of desires, you must take into consideration all of the elements of Desire noted in the above definite statement—the indirect as well as the direct elements of personal satisfaction and content.

You must weigh and decide the value of any particular desire, or class of desires, not only in the light of your own *immediate* satisfaction and content, but also in the light of your *own future* satisfaction and content; not only in the light of your own *direct* satisfaction and content, but also in the light of your *indirect* satisfaction and content derived from the satisfaction and content of others in whom you are interested. Your future satisfaction and content often depend upon the sacrifice of your present desire in favor of one bearing fruit in the future. You may be so interested in other persons that their satisfaction and content has a greater emotional value to you than the gratification of some desire concerned only with your own direct satisfaction and content. These Desires-values must be carefully weighed by you. If you leave out any of these elements of Desire, you run the risk of attaching a false value to certain sets of desires. You must weigh and measure the value of your desires by the use of the standard of the full content of Desire.

III. *Seek Depth of Desire.* You will find it advisable to omit from your list all purely superficial and transient feelings, emotions and desires. They have but a slight value in the case. Instead, plunge into the deep places of your mental being or soul; there you will find abiding certain deep, essential, basic, permanent feelings, emotions and desires. In those regions dwell the "wants" and the "want tos" which when aroused are as insistent and as imperative as are the want of the suffocating man for air; the want of the famished man for food; the want of the thirsting man for water; the want of the wild creature for its mate; the want of the mother for the welfare of her child.

These deep desires are your real emotional elements— the ones most firmly and permanently imbedded in the soil of your emotional being. These are the desires which will abide when the transient, ephemeral ones have passed and are forgotten. These are the desires for which you will be willing to "pay the price," be that price ever so high in the form of the sacrifice and relinquishment of every other desire, feeling or emotion. Measure your desires by their essential depth, as well as by their temporary weight. Select those which are embedded so deeply in the soil of your emotional being that they cannot be uprooted by the passing storms of conditions and circumstances.

The Struggle for Existence. You are now approaching the final stages of your discovery of "just what you want." You now have a list of Insistent Desires—the survivors in the Struggle for Existence on the part of your many desires and classes of desires. If you have proceeded earnestly and honestly in your work of Self-Analysis and Selection, you will have a group of sturdy Desire-giants before you for final judgment. By a strange psychological law these surviving candidates have taken on much of the strength and energy of those which they have defeated in the struggle; the victors will have absorbed the vitality of those whom they have defeated, just as the savage hopes to draw to himself the strength of the enemies killed by him in battle. Your Desire Power has now been concentrated upon a comparatively small group of desires, with a consequent focusing of power.

You will now find that your "wants" and "want tos" have arranged themselves into two great classes, viz., (1) the great class of those desires which while *different* from other desires, or classes of desires, are not necessarily *contradictory* to them nor *directly opposed* to them; and (2) the great class of those desires which are not only *different*, but are also actually *contradictory* and *opposed* to other desires or classes of desires.

The merely *"different"* classes may abide in mutual harmonious existence and relation with or to each other, just as do light and heat, or the color and odor of a flower. But two *contradictory* and *opposing* classes of desires cannot co-exist and coordinate their energies in the same individual; both remaining in the fore, there will be friction, inharmony, strife, and mutual interference.

One might as well try to ride two horses moving in different directions, as to try to maintain in equal force two opposing or contradictory sets of desires. The two sets, each one pulling in an opposite direction and with equal strength, will bring the Will to a standstill. The individual, in such a case, will either oscillate between the two attracting poles, or else he will come to a "dead center" between them. Something must be done when you find an opposing set of desires of this kind well to the fore in your category of strong desires. You must set in operation a process of competition, from which one set must emerge a victor and the other set be defeated.

In this process of competition, you will need to employ your best and keenest powers of analysis and judgment. In some cases the matter may be settled quickly, and the decision easily arrived at, because when your full attention is turned upon the two competitors, one will be seen to stand out so much more clearly than the other that the latter will be almost automatically retired. The full power of Reason and Feeling focused in such a case will usually result in a quick and sure decision.

But there are instances in which both of the opposing sets of desires seem to possess an equal power and value in your emotional and intellectual scale. Here you are apparently in the condition of the poor donkey, previously mentioned, who starved to death because he was unable to decide which of the two haystacks was to be eaten. The matter must be decided by the introduction of an additional element which will add weight to one set or the other, and thus bring down the balance on that particular side. This added element is usually found in one or the other of the following two classes of mental processes, viz., (1) Imagination, and (2) Association. Let us consider each of these.

The Element of Imagination. The imagination, employed in the case of the desire-conflict now before us, usually is very effective in bringing about a decision. In employing it, you have but to imagine yourself, first, in the actual possession of the object of the one set of desires; and then, instead, in possession of the object of the second set. In this process you draw upon your own recollections and experiences, and upon your recollection of the experiences of others. You imagine "how it would feel" to have attained the object of, first, *this* "want" or "want to," and then *that* one. You place yourself in imagination in the position that you would occupy in case you should attain the object of *this* desire, or of *that* one. Then you pass judgment as to which seems to be the better, i.e., to afford the greater degree of satisfaction and content, present and future, direct and indirect.

This process has the advantage of overcoming the handicap placed upon a future satisfaction in favor of a present one. The future experience is brought into the field of the present, and thus may be compared with a present experience relieved of the handicap of time. This is a matter of great importance, for ordinarily the present-time value of an emotional feeling or desire is far greater than that of a past-time or future-time value of a similar experience. The test of imagination usually results in (1) strengthening the present value of a really advantageous emotional feeling and desire, and (2) in weakening the present value of an apparently advantageous, but really disadvantageous, one. The use of the memory and the imagination is to be highly recommended in the task of deciding the real and actual value of an emotional state or desire.

The Element of Association. The element of association introduced into a desire-conflict will often result speedily in a determination and decision in favor of one side as against the other. Association will add strength to one set of desires, and will weaken the opposing set, in most cases. The Association of Ideas is that psychological law which binds one set of ideas, or mental states, to others; so that by bringing one set into consciousness we tend to bring there also the associated sets. In the present case we bring into consciousness the associated consequences of each set of desires.

You may proceed to apply the test of Association as follows: Seek to uncover and discover as many as possible of the associated results of the attainment of the set of desires in question—strive to think of "what else will happen" in case you attain that set of desires. This is something like inquiring into the family and social connections of two rival suitors or sweethearts—weighing their respective relations and associations and the probable future consequences of marriage with either of them.

It is always well, in cases of doubt concerning the comparative value of conflicting sets of desires, to consider carefully just what other things are associated with each of the two respective sets of desires—just what other results are likely to accompany the attainment of the object or end of each set of desires under consideration. In other words, you should ascertain the kind of relations and friends possessed by each of the rival suitors or sweethearts. In this way you will often find that one of the two apparently equal sets of desires has some very agreeable and advantageous relations and associates, while the other has some very disagreeable and disadvantageous ones.

You thus discover, figuratively speaking "just what kind of family you are marrying into"; and you thus take stock of the respective associated and related "in laws," friends, associates and entanglements of each of the suitors. This is of great value, since in spite of the oft asserted statement that "I am not marrying the whole family," one usually really does do just that very thing.

The idea of the application of the test of Association in such cases may be expressed in a few words, as follows: The real test of any particular desire depends not alone upon the immediate results likely to accompany its attainment, but also upon the associated and related results which follow in its train of association and correlation—the results which necessarily "go with it," and which are so closely bound up with it that they cannot easily be detached from it. In some cases, the test of Association will reveal the fact that the price of the attainment of a certain set of desires is excessive—often actually prohibitive. In other cases, on the contrary, you will find by this test that you are getting a great bargain by reason of the "extras" which go with the thing itself. The objects of some desires are thus found to be "damaged goods"; while those of others are found to have an associative value not apparent to the casual observer.

An Appeal to the Touchstone. In cases in which careful analysis, deliberation, the tests of imagination and association, and all other means of weighing and measuring, trying and testing, fail to reveal the advantage of one set of desires over the opposing set, resort must be had to the Touchstone of Positivity so often referred to in this instruction. The Touchstone by which the Positivity of any mental state, thought, feeling, desire or action is determined is as follows: *"Will this tend to make me stronger, better and more efficient?"* In the degree that any mental state meets the requirements of this test, so is its degree of Positivity and consequent desirability.

In testing two sets of conflicting desires in this way, you ask yourself: *"Which of these two desires, if attained, will tend to make me stronger, better and more efficient?"* This is the Test Question. The answer should represent your final decision in the matter. The Touchstone is your Court of Last Resort, to be appealed to when all other tests have failed. Its report represents the best, highest and most valuable elements, mental, moral and spiritual, within your nature; all that is worst in you is absent therefrom. It represents your Summum Bonum—your Chief Good.

The Survival of the Fittest. By this time, your list of desires has resolved itself into a schedule or inventory of a few strong, dominant, prime desires, and of a larger number of lesser ones. The strongest desires should be finally tested in order to discover whether they are merely "different" from each other, or whether they are essentially mutually antagonistic and contradictory.

If they come under the latter category, then they must be pitted against each other until one of the pair wins the victory, and one goes down in defeat; for two sets of this kind must not be permitted to dwell permanently in your region of Desire: "a house divided against itself shall not stand." There must be fought a fight to the finish. One of the opposing sets must be rolled in the dust, while the other stands proudly erect as the victor. The defeated one, thereafter, must be compelled to say, "After you, monsieur," as our French cousins politely express it.

If two sets of desires are merely "different,'" and are not essentially and necessarily conflicting and antagonistic, then they may be permitted to remain dwelling in mutual peace and harmony, at least for the time being. This permission, however, is conditioned by the fact that there must not be too many of such sets occupying the front seats of Desire at the same time. The tendency should always be in the direction of concentration and focused energy; you should beware of scattered power and energy arising from a great diversity of desires and aims.

If you discover that there are too many strong "different" desires left after you have reached this stage of selection and elimination, you should carefully weigh each remaining set, subjecting it to the tests of memory, imagination, association and rational judgment, discarding all that are not found profitable and sufficiently advantageous. If you find that any of your desires cost you more than you get out of them; get rid of all those which do not pay for their keep."

Continue until you have left only a comparatively few sets of desires, all of proved value and superlative emotional strength and depth. These should be recognized as well worth the price which you are prepared to pay for their maintenance and support. Treat in the same way any new desires which arise within you. Test them just as you have tested their predecessors, and insist that they prove that they are "worth while" before you decide to keep them. If they cost you more than you get out of them, discard them. Insist that they shall "pay their keep" and yield you some emotional profit beside. Run your emotional and desire establishment on business principles.

You have now finally reached the stage in which you have on your list nothing but your Dominant Desires—the survivors in the Struggle for Existence—the Survival of the Fittest. These Dominant Desires must thereafter rule your emotional realm. Any new comer must prove its worth by a test of strength with these Dominant Desires—if it shows its strength, and is able to hold its place, very well; it may be added to the list. Those going down in defeat must be eliminated. This will require strength and determination on your part—but you are a strong and determined individual, or at least are becoming one.

The process of Self-Analysis and Selection which you just considered will furnish you with two classes of reports, viz., (1) it will demonstrate to you your strongest classes of desires—your Dominant Desires; and (2) it will cause you clearly and definitely to picture and form a strong idea of each of such

Dominant Desires. In both reports it will cause you to "know exactly what you want," which is the first requisite of the Master Formula of Attainment.

PUTTING POWER INTO YOUR DESIRE

According to the Master Formula you must not only "know exactly what you want," but must also "want it hard enough," and be "willing to pay the price of its attainment." Having considered the first of the above stated three requisites for obtaining that which you want, we ask you now to consider the second requisite, i.e., that of "wanting it hard enough."

You may think that you "want it hard enough" when you have a rather keen desire or longing for anything, but when you compare your feeling with that of persons manifesting really strong, insistent desire, you will find that you are but merely manifesting a "wish" for that for which you have an inclination or an attachment. Compared to the insistent "want" or "want to" of thoroughly aroused Desire, your "wish" is but as a shadow. The chances are that you have been a mere amateur—a dilettante—in the art and science of "wanting" and "wanting to." Very few persons really know how to "want" or "want to" in such manner as to arouse fully the elemental forces of Desire Power.

An old Oriental fable illustrates the nature of Desire aroused to its fullest extent. The fable relates that a teacher took his pupil out on a deep lake, in a boat, and then suddenly pushed him overboard. The youth sank beneath the surface of the water, but rose in a few seconds, gasping for breath. Without giving him time to fill his lungs with air, the teacher forcibly pushed him under once more. The youth rose to the surface the second time, and was again pushed under. He rose for the third time, almost entirely exhausted; this time the teacher pulled him up over the side of the boat, and employed the usual methods to restore him to normal breathing.

When the youth had fully recovered from his severe ordeal, the teacher said to him: "Tell me what was the one thing that you desired above all other things before I pulled you in—the one desire to which all other desires seem like tiny candles compared with the sun?" The youth replied, "Oh, sir; above all else I desired air to breathe—for me at that time there existed no other desires!" Then said the teacher, "Let this, then, be the measure of your desire for those things to the attainment of which your life is devoted!"

You will not fully realize the measure of Desire pointed out in this fable, unless you employ your imagination in the direction of feeling yourself in the drowning condition of the youth—until you do this, the fable is a mere matter of words. When you can realize in feeling, as well as recognize in thought, the strength of the desire for air present in that youth, then, and then only, will you be able to manifest in expression a similar degree of Desire for the objects of your prime "wants" and "want tos." Do not rest satisfied with the intellectual recognition of the condition—induce the corresponding emotional feeling in yourself to as great a degree as possible.

Varying the illustration, you will do well to induce in yourself (in imagination) the realization of the insistent, paramount desire for food experienced by the starving man lost in the dense forest in mid-winter. The chances are that you never have been actually "hungry" in the true sense of the term; all that you have mistaken for hunger is merely the call of appetite or taste—the result of habit. When you are so hungry that an old, stale, dry crust of bread will be delicious to your taste, then you are beginning to know what real hunger is. Those men who, lost in the forest or shipwrecked, have tried to satisfy intense hunger by gnawing the bark of trees, or chewing bits of leather cut from their boots—these men could give you some interesting information concerning hunger. If you can imagine the feelings of men in this condition, then you may begin to understand what "insistent desire" really means.

Again, the shipwrecked sailors adrift at sea with their supply of water exhausted; or the desert-lost man wandering over the hot sands with a thirst almost inconceivable to the ordinary person; those men know what "insistent desire" means. Man can live many days without food; but only a few days without water; and only a few minutes without air. When these fundamental essentials of life are withdrawn temporarily, the living creature finds his strongest and most elemental feelings and desires aroused— they become transmuted into passions insistently demanding satisfaction and content. When these elemental emotions and desires are thoroughly aroused, all the derivative emotional states are forgotten. Imagine the emotional state of the starving man in sight of food, or the thirst-cursed man within reach of water, if some other person or thing intervenes and attempts to frustrate the suffering man's attainment of that which he wants above all else at that time.

Other examples of insistent desire may be found in the cases of wild animals in the mating season, in which they will risk life and defy their powerful rivals in order to secure the chosen mate. If you ever have come across a bull-moose in the mating season, you will have a vivid picture and idea of this phase of elemental desire raised to the point of "insistent demand."

Again, consider the intense emotional feeling, and the accompanying desires experienced by the mother creature in connection with the welfare and protection of her young when danger threatens them—this will show you the nature and character of elemental desire aroused to its fullest extent. Even tiny birds will fight against overwhelming odds in resisting the animal or man seeking to rob their nests. It is a poor spirited mother-animal which will not risk her life, and actually court death, in defense of her young. The female wild creature becomes doubly formidable when accompanied by her young. "The female of the species" is far "more deadly than the male" when the welfare of its young is involved. The Orientals have a proverb: "It is a very brave, or a very foolish, man who will try to steal a young tiger-cub while its mother is alive and free in the vicinity."

We have called your attention to the above several examples and illustrations of the force of strongly aroused elemental emotions and desires, not alone to point out to you how powerful such desires and feelings become under the appropriate circumstances and conditions, but also to bring you to a realization of the existence within all living things of a latent emotional strength and power which is capable of being aroused into a strenuous activity under the proper stimulus, and of being directed toward certain definite ends and purposes indicated by the stimulus. That this strength and power is aroused by, and flows out toward, the particular forms of stimulus above indicated is a matter of common knowledge. But that it may be aroused to equal strength, power, and intensity by other forms of stimulus (such stimulus having been deliberately placed before it by the individual) is not known to the many; only the few have learned this secret.

We ask you to use your imagination here, once more, for a moment. Imagine an individual who has "his mind set upon" the attainment of a certain end or purpose to such a degree that he has aroused the latent Desire Power within him to that extent where he "wants" or "wants to" that end or purpose in the degree of strength, power, insistency and fierceness, manifested by the drowning man who "wants" air; by the desert lost man who "wants" water; by the starving man who wants food; by the wild creature who "wants" its mate; by the mother animal who "wants" the welfare of its young. This is the individual in whom the elemental Desire Power has been aroused to such an extent, and directed toward the attainment or achievement of his Dominant Desire. How would you like to compete with such a man for the attainment of that object of his Desire Power? How would you like to be the opposing obstacle standing directly in his path of progress and attainment? How would you like to play with him the part analogous to that of one who would try to snatch away the bone from a starving wolf, or pull the tiger cub from the paws of its savage mother?

This is an extreme case or illustration, of course. Very few individuals actually reach the stage indicated—though it is not impossible by any means; but many travel a long way along that road. The strong, successful men who have "made good," who have "arrived," who have "done things," in any line of human endeavor, will be found to have travelled quite a distance in that direction, on the road of Desire. They have aroused within themselves the strong, elemental Desire Power which abides in latency in the depths of the mental and emotional being—the "soul," if you will—of every human creature; and have caused that elemental force to pour through the channels of the particular Dominant Desires which they have brought to the surface of their nature from the depths of the subconscious self.

Look in any direction you may, and you will find that the strong, masterful, dominant, successful men are those in whom Desire Power has been aroused and directed in this way. These men "know what they want"—just as the drowning man, the starving man, the thirst-cursed man, the wild mating creature, the mother creature, each knows what he or she wants—they have no doubts concerning their Dominant Desires. And these men also "want hard enough" that which represents their Dominant Desires—just as did the drowning man, the starving man, and the rest of our illustrative examples. And, like those examples, these men were also "willing to pay the price."

Run over the list of the successful men and women with whose careers you are acquainted. Place on that list the great discoverers, inventors, explorers, military men, business men, artists, literary men and women, all those who have "done things" successfully. Then check off name after name, as you discover the biographical report of the Desire Power manifested by these individuals. You will find that in each and every case there were present the "Definite Ideals, Insistent Desire, Confident Expectation, Persistent Determination, and Balanced Compensation," which constitute the Master Formula of Attainment of our instruction. And this second requisite—the "Insistent Desire"—is found to be this elemental Desire Power directed into the appropriate channels of manifestation and expression. These individuals "knew just what they wanted"; they "wanted it hard enough"; and they were "willing to pay the price."

It is this spirit of "wanting it hard enough" that distinguishes the men and women of strong purpose and determination from the common herd of persons who merely "wish for" things in a gentle, faint, conventional way—that distinguishes the true "wanters" from the dilettante "wishers." It was the recognition of this spirit in men that caused Disraeli to say that long meditation had brought him to the conviction that a human being with a settled purpose, and with a will which would stake even existence itself upon its fulfillment, must certainly accomplish that purpose.

"But," you may say, "admitting the truth of your premise, how am I to proceed in order to arouse the dormant latent Desire Power within me, and to cause it to flow forth in the direction of the attainment of my Dominant Desires?" Answering the question, we would say, "Begin at the very beginning, and proceed to arouse and draw forth the latent Desire Power, by presenting to it the stimulus of suggestive and inciting ideas and pictures." For, from beginning to end, there prevails the principle expressed in that axiom of psychology which says: *"Desire is aroused and flows forth toward things represented by ideas and mental pictures; the stronger and clearer the idea or mental picture, the stronger and more insistent is the aroused desire, all else being equal."*

You should proceed to apply this principle from the very beginning even at the stage of semi-awakened Desire Power. There abides within you a great store of latent, dormant Desire Power—a great reservoir of Desire Power which is almost dormant, but which contains within itself the latent and nascent powers of wonderfully diversified manifestation and expression. You will do well to begin by "stirring up" this great reservoir of Desire Power—arousing it into activity in a general way, to the end that you may afterward direct its power and cause it to flow forth into and along the channels of expression and manifestation which you have provided for it.

In the great crater of a mighty volcano of Hawaii, in plain sight of the daring visitor to the rim of the abyss, there abides a large lake of molten lava, seething and bubbling, boiling and effervescing in a state of hissing ebullience—a lake of liquid fire, as it were. This great fiery lake is comparatively calm on its surface, however, the ebullition proceeding from its depths. The whole body of fiery liquid manifests a rhythmic tide-like rise and fall, and a swaying from side to side of the crater. The observer is impressed with the recognition of a latent and nascent power of almost immeasurable possibilities of manifestation and expression. He feels borne upon him the conviction that this seething, rising and falling, swaying, tremendous body of liquid fire, if once fully aroused into activity, would boil and seethe up to the edge of the crater, and overflowing, would pour down into the valleys beneath carrying before it and destroying every obstacle in its path.

This great lake of molten lava—this great body of liquid fire—is a symbol of the great body of latent and nascent Desire Power abiding within every individual—within YOU. It rests there, comparatively inactive on the surface, but ever manifesting a peculiar churning ebullition proceeding from its great depths. It seethes and boils, effervesces and bubbles, rises and falls in tide-like rhythm, sways in rhythmic sequence from side to side. It seems ever to say to you, "I am here, restless and disturbed, ever longing, craving, hankering for, hungering and thirsting for, desiring for expression and manifestation in definite form and direction. Stir me up; arouse my inner force; set me into action; and I will rise and assert my power, and accomplish for you that which you direct!"

Of course, we realize that this stirring up or agitation of your latent Desire Power is apt to—in fact, certainly will— create additional Discontent on your part; but what of it? Some philosophers praise the Spirit of Contentment, and say that Happiness is to be found only therein. Be that as it may, it may be as positively asserted that all Progress proceeds from Discontent.

While admitting the value of Content, at the same time we believe in preaching the "Gospel of Discontent" to a sane degree and extent. We believe that Discontent is the first step on the Path of Attainment. We believe that it is just this very Divine Discontent that causes men and women to undertake the Divine Adventure of Life, and which is back of and under all human progress. Content may be carried quite too far. Absolute Content results in Apathy and Lethargy—it stops the wheels of Progress. Nature evidently is not Content, else it would cease to manifest the process of Evolution. Nature has evidently been ever filled with the Spirit of Discontent, judging from her invariable manifestation of the Law of Change. Without Discontent and the Desire to Change, there would be no Change in Nature. The Law of Change shows plainly Nature's opinion on the subject, and her prevailing feelings and desires in the matter.

You will do well to begin by "treating" your great body of elemental Desire Power for increased activity, and for the transmutation of its static power into dynamic power— bringing it from its state of semi-rest into the state of increased restlessness and tendency to flow forth into action. You may do this in the same way that you will later employ in the case of specific, particular and definite desires, i.e., *by presenting to it suggestive and inciting ideas and mental pictures!*

Begin by presenting to your elemental Desire Power the suggestive idea and mental picture of itself as akin to the great lake of molten lava, or liquid fire, filled with latent and nascent energy, power and force; filled with the elemental urge toward expression and manifestation in outward form and action; able and willing to accomplish anything it desires to do with sufficient strength, providing a definite channel is provided for its flow of power. Show it the picture of itself as ready and willing to transmute its static energy into dynamic force, and to pour forth along the channels which you will provide for it—and above all else, quite *able* to do this if it will but arouse itself into dynamic action. In short, present to its gaze your idealistic and ideative mental equipment in the form of the surface of a great mirror, reflecting the picture of the elemental Desire Power as it presents itself to that mirror—let Desire Power see itself as it is. Supply Desire with its complementary Idea.

You will do well to accompany this mental picture with a verbal statement or affirmation of the details of that picture. Treat your elemental Desire Power as if it were an entity— there is a valid psychological reason for this, by the way—and tell it in exact words just what it is, what are its powers, and what is its essential nature displaying the disposition to express and manifest itself in outward form and activity. Pound these suggestive statements into it, as firmly, earnestly and persistently as you can. Supply the Desire Power with the element of Idea and Mental Pictures. Give it the picture of what it is, and the pattern or diagram of what it can do if it will.

The result of this course of "treatment" applied to your elemental Desire Power will soon show itself in an increased feeling of more vigorous rhythmic tidal-movement and side-to-side movement, as previously described; and in an increased rate and vigor of its seething, boiling, effervescing ebullition. From its depths 'will arise mighty impulses and urges, upheavals and uprisings. The great molten-lake of Desire Power will begin to boil with increased vigor, and will show an inclination to produce the Steam of Will. You will experience new and strange evidences of the urge of Desire Power within you, seeking expression and manifestation along the channels which you have provided for it.

But before reaching this stage, you must have created the channels through and in which you wish the overflowing Desire Power to flow when it reaches the "boiling over" stage. These channels must be built along the lines of those desires which you have proved to be your Dominant Desires. Build these channels, deep, wide and strong. From them you can afterward build minor channels for your secondary and derivative desires arising from your Dominant Desires. At present, however, your main concern is with your main channels. Let each channel represent the clear, deep, strong idea and mental picture of "just what you want" as you clearly see and know it. You have found out exactly what you want, when you want it, and how you want it; let your channels represent as closely as may be just these ideas. Build the banks high, so as to obviate any waste; build the walls strong, so as to stand the strain; build the channel deep and wide, so as to carry the full force and quantity of the current.

By "creating the channels" of your Dominant Desires, we mean establishing the paths to be traversed by the overflowing current of Desire Power which you have aroused from its latent and nascent condition. These channels or paths are created mentally by the employment of Creative Imagination and Ideation. These mental forces proceed to manifest in the direction of creating and presenting to your consciousness the ideas and mental pictures of your Dominant Desires which you have discovered in your process of Self-Analysis. The work of creating these channels is really but a continuation of the mental work performed by you in the discovery of your Dominant Desires. In creating these channels you should observe three general rules, as follows:

(1) *Make the Channels Clear and Clean* by creating and maintaining a clear, clean, distinct, and definite idea of each of your Dominant Desires, in which idea the entire thought concerning the Dominant Desire is condensed, and in which there is no foreign or non-essential material.

(2) *Make the Channels Deep and Wide* by forming mental pictures or suggestive ideas appealing to the emotional feelings associated with the Dominant Desires, and thus tempting the appetites of those desires by the representation of the objects of their longing, and by the presentation of imaginative pictures of the joys which will attend their final achievement and attainment.

(3) *Make the Banks Strong* by means of the employment of the Persistent Determination of the Will, so that the powerful swift current may be confined within the limits of the Dominant Desire and not be permitted to escape and waste itself by scattering its energy and force over the surrounding land.

When your current is flowing freely, you will find it necessary to build minor channels serving to bring about the attainment of objects and ends helpful to the accomplishment of the objects and ends of the major channels. In building these minor channels, follow the same general rules and principles which we have given you. From the great main channels down to the tiniest canal the same principle is involved. *Always build clear and clean, by means of definite ideas and aims; always build deep and wide, by means of suggestive ideas and mental pictures; always build strong banks, by means of the determined will.*

In concluding this consideration of the second requisite, i.e., the element of "wanting it hard enough," we wish to impress upon your mind the tremendous vitalizing, and inciting power exerted by Suggestive Ideas and Mental Pictures upon Desire Power. Suggestive Ideas and Mental Pictures act upon Desire Power with a tremendous degree of effect in the direction of inciting, arousing, stirring, stimulating, exciting, spurring, goading, provoking, moving, encouraging, animating and urging to expression and manifestation. There are no other incentives equal to these. All strong desires are aroused by such incentives, consciously or unconsciously applied.

For instance, you may have no desire to visit California. Then your interest in that part of the country is aroused by what you read or hear concerning it, and a vague desire to visit it is aroused in you. Later, information in the direction of giving you additional material for suggestive ideas and mental pictures serves to arouse your desire to "go to California." You begin to search eagerly for further ideas and pictures, and the more you obtain the stronger grows the flame of your desire. At last, you "want to hard enough," and brushing aside all obstacles you "pay the price" and take the trip across the plains. Had you not been furnished with the additional suggestive ideas and mental pictures, your original desire would soon have died out. You know by experience the truth of this principle; you also know how you would use it if you wished to induce a friend to visit California, do you not? Then start to work using it on your Desire Power when you wish to incite it into "wanting hard enough" something that you know to be advantageous to you!

It is customary to illustrate this principle by the figure of pouring the oil of Idea upon the flame of Desire, thereby keeping alive and strengthening the power of the latter. The figure of speech is a good one—the illustration serves well its purpose. But your memory and imagination, representing your experience, will furnish you with one a little nearer home. All that you need do is to imagine the effect which would be produced upon you if you were hungry and were able to form the mental picture or create the suggestive idea of a particularly appetizing meal. Even as it is, though you are not really hungry, the thought of such a meal will make your mouth water.

Again, you may readily imagine the effect produced upon you, when you are parched and intensely thirsty on a long ride, by the vivid mental picture or strong suggestive idea of a clear, cold spring of mountain water. Or, again, when in a stuffy, ill-ventilated office you think of the fresh air of the mountain-camp where you went fishing last Summer,—when you picture plainly the joys of the experience—can you deny that your Desire Power is intensely aroused and excited, and that you feel like dropping everything and "taking to the woods" at once.

Raising the principle to its extreme form of manifestation, try to imagine the effect upon the famishing man of a dream of plentiful food; the dream of the thirst-cursed man in which is pictured flowing fountains of water. Try to imagine the effect upon the mate-seeking wild bull-moose of the far-off bellow of the sought-for mate—would you like to impede his path on such an occasion. Finally, picture the emotional excitement and frenzy of desire on the part of the tigress when she comes in sight of food for her half-starved cubs;

or her force of desire when she hears afar-off the cry of distress of her young ones.

In order to "want" and "want to" as hard as do these human beings and wild things which we have employed as illustrations, you must feed your Desire Power with suggestive ideas and mental pictures similar in exciting power to those which rouse into action their dominant and paramount "want" and "want to." Of course, these are extreme cases—but they serve to illustrate the principle involved.

In short, in order to "want it hard enough," you must create a gnawing hunger and a parching thirst for the objects of your Dominant Desires; this you must intensify and render continuous by repeatedly presenting with suggestive ideas and mental pictures of the Feast of Good Things, and the Flowing Fountain, which awaits the successful achievement or attainment of the desires.

Or, you must be like the half-drowned youth wanting "a breath of air" above all else—wanting it with all the fierce energy of his soul and being; and you must ever keep before you the suggestive idea and mental picture of "all the air there is" which is to be found just above the surface of the water of Need in which you are now immersed. When you can create these mental and emotional conditions within yourself, then, and then only, will you really know just what it is to "want hard enough."

Think well over this idea, until you grasp its full meaning!

HOW TO OVERCOME TEMPTATIONS THAT SIDETRACK YOUR AMBITIONS

According to the Master Formula, "In order to get what you want you must not only know exactly what you want," not only "want it hard enough," but also "be willing to pay the price of its attainment." We have considered the first and second of these elements of successful attainment; let us now consider the third one, and learn what it means to "be willing to pay the price of attainment."

This final element of successful attainment—this last hurdle in the race—often is the point at which many persons fail; riding gallantly over the first several hurdles, they stumble and fall when they attempt to surmount this final one. This, not so much because of the real difficulty in passing over this obstacle, but rather because they are apt to underestimate the task and, accordingly, to relax their energies. Thinking that the race is practically over, they fail to observe care and caution and thus meet failure. With the prize almost in hand, they relax their efforts and lose it.

The Law of Compensation is found in full operation in the realm of Desire, as well as in every other field and region of life and action. There is always present that insistence upon Balance which Nature invariably demands from those who seek her prizes. There is always something to be given up, in order that something else may be gained. One cannot have his pie and his dime at the same time—he must spend the dime if he would buy the pie. Neither can one keep his dime and yet spend it. Nature boldly and plainly displays her sign, "Pay the Price!" Once more let us quote the old adage: "Said the gods to man, 'Take what thou wilt; but pay the price.'"

When in actual experience you perform the process of selection of the Dominant Desires, with its attendant Struggle for Existence and Survival of the Fittest among the competing desires, even then you are beginning to "pay the price" of the attainment of your Dominant Desires; this because you are setting aside and relinquishing one or more sets of desires in favor of a preferred set. Every set of desires has its opposing set, and also others sets which would to some extent interfere with its full manifestation; you must "pay the price" of attainment of the one set of desires by relinquishing the other sets.

In order to attain the object of your desire for wealth, you must "pay the price" of relinquishing desires for certain things which would prevent you from accumulating money. In order to attain the object of your desire for all possible knowledge in some particular field of study and research, you must "pay the price" of relinquishing your desires for a similar degree of knowledge in some other field of thought and study. In order to attain the object of your desire for business success, you must "pay the price" of hard work and the passing by of the objects of your desires for play, amusement, and enjoyment which would necessitate the neglect of your business. And so on; to attain the object of any one set of desires, you must always "pay the price" of the relinquishing of the objects of other sets of desires.

In some cases, this process of the inhibition of opposing desires is akin to that of weeding your garden, or of pruning your trees—getting rid of the useless and harmful growths which interfere with the growth and development of the useful and advantageous thing. In other cases, however, the desires which you must inhibit and put away from you are not in themselves harmful or useless. On the contrary, they may be very advantageous and useful in themselves, and may be actually worthy of being adopted as Dominant Desires by others; but, at the same time, they are of such a nature as to prove an obstacle to your progress along the line of your own chosen Dominant Desires.

Things may oppose and antagonize each other without either of them being harmful or "bad" in themselves. You cannot travel at the same time both forks of the road; nor can you travel north and south on any road at the same time; though either of these courses of travel may be good in itself. You cannot very well be a successful clergyman and a successful lawyer at the same time; if you have strong desires for both of these careers, you must choose the one you desire more and set aside the other. The girl with the two attractive suitors—the man with the two delightful sweethearts—the child with the dime, gazing longingly at the two different tarts—each must choose one and pass by the other, and thus "pay the price."

Not only in the preliminary process of discovering and identifying your Dominant Desires are you called upon to "pay the price," but you are equally called upon to do so at almost every subsequent step and stage of your progress in actual experience. There is always something presenting itself to tempt you into "sidetracking" your Desire Power; some alluring desires which beckon you from the straight Path of Attainment. Here you will find that it is hard to "pay the price"; and often you will gravely question yourself, asking if the things represented by the Dominant Desires are, after all, worth the price you are being called on to pay for them. These temptations and struggles come to all— they constitute one of the tests whereby it is determined whether you are strong or whether you are weak in regard to your Desire Power. Here is the real test of whether or not you "want it hard enough" to make you willing to "pay the price."

Particularly difficult to overcome and conquer are those temptations which induce you to relinquish your desire for future attainment in favor of the gratification of present desires; or which tempt you to forego the attainment of permanent future benefits in favor of temporary, ephemeral benefits. The tempter whispers in your ear that you are foolish to content yourself with the skim-milk of the present in the hope of obtaining the full cream of tomorrow. The ever-present suggestion to "Eat, drink, and be merry, for tomorrow we die" must be boldly confronted and conquered if you wish to attain the object of that which your reason and judgment, as well as your self-analysis, has shown that you really want above everything else. The habit of saying: "Get thee behind me Satan!" must be cultivated; and when you have got him behind you, look out lest he give you a push from behind!

Here you determine whether or not you really "want it hard enough." The drowning man is in no doubt concerning the value of the breath of air. He is willing to "pay the price of it," no matter how high that price may be. The famishing man knows the value of food—the parched man knows the value of water: they are willing to "pay the price," and are not liable to be sidetracked from their Dominant Desire. The bull-moose seeking his mate is willing to "pay the price" of danger and possible death lying in his path— but you cannot sidetrack him. The mother tiger cannot be sidetracked from the pursuit of food for her hungry cubs— she is willing to "pay the price" of risk of life without hesitation. When you begin to "want it hard enough" along the same lines, and reaching toward the same degree of intensity and insistence manifested by these creatures, then you will not hesitate to "pay the price"—to pay it in full, and without hesitation; when you reach this stage the tempter will whisper into ears deaf to his voice.

In order to hold the current of Desire Power within the bounds of your channels of Dominant Desire, the banks must be erected and kept in a state of strength by Will Power. The "Will to Will" must be called into manifestation. While Desire is one of the fundamental elements of Will, it is not all of Will. Will is a subtle combination of Conative Desire and of Purposeful Determination. It springs from Desire, but it evolves into something which is capable of mastering Desire by its power of "Willing to Will."

Here follow three general rules which you should note very carefully in connection with the subject of inhibiting and setting-aside the temptations of conflicting desires—of those desires which are constantly springing up and tempting you to forego "paying the price," or to become "sidetracked" from the Path of Attainment of your Dominant Desires. Two of these rules are along the lines of which we have spoken in connection with the influence of Representative Ideas upon Desire Power.

I. Under temptation by sidetracking desires, use every effort to feed the Flame of Desire of your Dominant Desires, by an increased supply of suggestive ideas and mental pictures tending to stimulate its heat and incite its energy.

II. At the same time, strenuously avoid feeding the flame of the tempting desires by suggestive ideas and mental pictures likely to arouse or incite them. On the contrary, carefully and positively refuse to admit such ideas and pictures to your mind so far as is possible; seek to starve the fires of such desires by withholding from them the fuel necessary for their continuance and support.

The third rule involves another psychological principle, and is as follows:

III. So far as is possible, transmute the sidetracking desires into forms more in accordance with general trend of the Dominant Desires, thereby converting them into helpful rather than harmful emotional energy.

In the case of the first rule above stated, you tend to inhibit the energy of the sidetracking desires by imparting additional energy to the Dominant Desires. When the attention is strongly attracted or held by the suggestive ideas and mental pictures of a strong set of desires, it is not easily diverted by those of a weaker set. The strong light of the former tend to cast the latter into a comparative shadow. The attention firmly concentrated and held upon one particular set of ideas and mental pictures refuses to accept the demand of another set. Keep the attention busy with the advantageous set, and it "will have no time" for the consideration of the opposing set. With these opposing suggestive ideas and mental pictures kept out of the field of conscious attention, the desires associated with them tend to die down and finally to disappear.

In the case of the second rule above stated you deliberately and determinedly refuse to feed the flame of the sidetracking desires with the fuel of suggestive ideas and mental pictures. Instead, you proceed deliberately and determinedly to starve that flame. No flame of desire can long continue to burn vigorously if its supply of suggestive fuel be cut off from it. Cut off the fuel supply of any desire, and it will begin to decrease in vigor and force. Refuse to allow your mind to dwell upon the ideas or mental pictures tending to suggest the sidetracking desires. When such ideas and pictures intrude themselves and seek to attract the attention, you must deliberately turn your attention to something else—preferably to the suggestive ideas and pictures of your Dominant Desires.

The Roman Catholic Church evidently recognizes the value of this rule, for its teachers instruct their pupils to form the habit of turning their attention to prayers and certain forms of devotional exercises when temptations assail them. The attention being directed to and held firmly upon the devotional exercise or ceremony, it is withheld from the suggestive ideas and mental pictures of the tempting desire; and, accordingly, the latter loses strength and in time dies away. Without detracting from the value of the religious element involved, we may say that it is certain that the purely psychological effect of such course is highly advantageous. You would do well to apply the principle in your own case.

In the case of the third rule above stated, you transmute the energy of the sidetracking desire into that of desires more in accordance with the general trend of your Dominant Desires. In this way you not only obviate the danger of the interference and distraction of the sidetracking desires, but also actually employ the basic energy of Desire Power to feed the flame of the advantageous desires. Here, the principle involved is not so well known as are those involved in the other rules; but that principle is sound, nevertheless, and is capable of being employed with remarkable results by the individual possessing sufficient will power and determination to apply it.

As an example of this principle of the transmutation of the form of Desire Force, let us point you to a fact well known to scientific observers, viz., that the energy of the sexual passions may be transmuted into the energy of any kind of mental or physical creative work. This fact is also known to priests and others who are called on for advice from those wishing to control passions of this kind. The explanation probably lies in the fact that sexual desire is essentially *creative* in its fundamental nature, and therefore is capable of being diverted to other forms of creative activity. But whatever may be the true explanation, it is a fact that the person experiencing strong intruding sexual desires may proceed to master and control them by means of engaging in some form of creative work in which the elemental creative energy is transmuted into other forms of creative force.

For instance, one may *create* by writing, musical composition, artistic work, or making and constructing things with the hands—in fact, by any kind of work in which things are made, put together, constructed or created in any way. In all of such work, provided that sufficient interest is thrown into the task, it will be found that the strong impulse of the intruding sexual passions will gradually lose its force, and that the person will then experience a sense of new energy in the creative work which he has undertaken in order to transmute the previous form of Desire Power.

The experienced physician knows that the best possible prescription for certain classes of cases of this kind coming to him for treatment and advice is that of "interesting work" for head or hands or both. There is much truth in the old saying that "An idle brain is the devil's workshop," and the similar one that "The devil finds plenty of work for idle hands to do." This principle may be set to work against "the devil," by simply reversing its action by giving head and hands plenty to do.

Another illustration of this principle is found in the case of the beneficial effect of certain games—in fact, of nearly all games played in moderation. Here the sidetracking and distracting desires which seek to take one away from his appointed tasks, and from the manifestation of his Dominant Desires, are transmuted into the interest, feeling, and desires of Play. Play is a safety-valve of emotional feeling. It serves to transmute many a distracting desire into the conative energy expressing itself in an interesting game. This is true of games involving purely mental skill, as well as those in which physical skill is also involved. Baseball has been a wonderful benefit to the American people in this way. Golf is playing an important part in the direction of affording a "transmutation channel" of energy for busy men who tire under the somewhat monotonous strain of the strenuous pursuit of the object of their Dominant Desires. In cases of this kind, not only are the distracting desires transmuted in this way, but the games themselves give recreation, exercise and a restful change of occupation to the individual.

"Paying the price" of your Dominant Desires does not necessarily imply that you must give up everything in life not actually concerned in furthering the interests of those particular desires—in such case, indeed, you would probably actually injure your own interests by too closely restricting your circle of interest and attention. The real meaning of the injunction is that you must "pay the price" of *giving up, inhibiting, or at least transmuting any and all desires which directly and certainly oppose and seriously interfere with the attainment of the objects of your Dominant Desires.* That price, indeed, you must be prepared to pay. In many cases, such desires may be transmuted into forms which will in a sense "run along with" the pursuit of the objects of your Dominant Desires, and thus be rendered helpful rather than harmful. Many emotional elements may be turned to account in this way by the process of transmutation. You should give some thought to this matter of transmutation when you are threatened by distracting and sidetracking desires.

Another form of "paying the price" is that of the labor and work to be performed by the individual in his task of attainment of the object of his Dominant Desires. This work and labor, however, is not alone performed by the exercise of the Persistent Determination of the Will, though this is the active element involved; there is needed also the inhibition and starving out of the conflicting or sidetracking desires which strive to draw the individual away from his appointed tasks and toward the actions requiring less work, and which for the time being seem to be richer in promise of pleasure and satisfaction.

The price paid by the men and women who have achieved marked success almost always is found to include self-denial, and sometimes even actual privation during the earlier days of the undertaking; work far in excess of that rightfully demanded of the wage earner, both in amount and in time is demanded of them; application and unwearied perseverance are required of them; indomitable resolution and persistent determination must be "paid" by them. There is here the constant giving up of the present pleasure in favor of that hoped for in the future. There is here the constant performance of tasks which might easily be avoided, and which are really avoided by the average person, but which are required to be performed by the individual who is inspired by the Dominant Desire and who is working for the accomplishment of "the one big thing."

Napoleon "paid the price" in his earlier days when he refused to indulge in the frivolous pursuits of his fellow-students at Brienne, and instead, deliberately devoted his spare time to the mastery of the elements of military science and history. Abraham Lincoln "paid the price" when he studied the few books he could find by the light of the fireplace, instead of indulging in the pleasures and dissipations of the other young men of his neighborhood. Read the history of any successful man and you will find this invariable "paying the price" of study, application, work, self-denial, economy, thrift, industry and the rest of the needful things.

Never delude yourself with the thought that you can escape "paying the price" of the attainment of the objects of your strong desires. The price must always be paid— the greater the object of attainment the greater is the price demanded. But you will find that if you have learned how to "want it hard enough" then the price will be comparatively easy to pay—the thing will be deemed well worth it.

If you feel that the price that you are being called upon to pay for the object of your Dominant Desires is more than the thing is worth, then there is something wrong about the whole matter. In such case, you should carefully "take stock" of your feelings, weighing and comparing them carefully as we have suggested in our consideration of Self-Analysis, and selection of Dominant Desires. You may find that what you had supposed to be a Dominant Desire is not really such at all. Or you may find that you have failed to include some necessary element or phase of the Dominant Desire. Or, that you have failed to make some possible transmutation of distracting desires; or have failed to inhibit or starve out sidetracking desires. Or, possibly, that you have failed to feed the flame of your Dominant Desire properly. At any rate, there is something wrong in such a case, and you should seek the remedy.

While the Law of Nature provides that you must "pay the price" of any and all desires, it also provides that the attainment must always be worth the price. If you find that the present and probable future value of any object of your desire is not worth the price you must be called upon to pay for it, then you should carefully consider the whole matter most critically, viewing it from all angles, and in the light of all possible relations and associations, with full deliberation concerning the probable consequences of an opposite course, and with thoughtful judgment concerning all alternative courses. The dissatisfaction may be merely temporary and passing, or on the other hand, it may be growing in strength and promise of permanency.

Any desire which upon careful consideration, deliberation, and judgment may seem not to "pay for its keep"—to be not worth its storage charges or floor space in your emotional nature—is a fit object for a final retrial upon its merits, a re-valuation of its points, in order to decide whether it shall be retained and treated for additional strength, energy and emotional value, or else discarded and rejected. The test should always be: *"Is this really worth while—worth the price I am called on to pay for it; would its rejection cost me more than its retention?"* The Touchstone of Merit should be: *"Does this render me stronger, better and more efficient—and, therefore, more truly and permanently happier?"*

SUMMARY

You have seen that Desire is that emotional state which is represented by the phrase, *"I want!"* You have seen that *"Desire has for its object something which will bring pleasure or get rid of pain, immediate or remote, for the individual or for some one in whom he is interested."* You have seen that *"You always act according to your greatest 'like' or 'dislike' of which you are cognizant at the time."* You have seen that *"The degree of force, energy, will, determination, persistence, and continuous application manifested by an individual in his aspirations, ambitions, aims, performances, actions and work is determined primarily by the degree of his desire for the attainment of the objects thereof—his degree of 'want' and 'want to' concerning that object."* You have seen that *"Desire is the Flame that produces the Steam of Will,"* and that, therefore, Desire is the source from which all human action springs.

You have seen that not only does Desire Power directly or indirectly cause all human action, but that it also sets into operation the Life Forces which develop the mental and physical faculties and powers of the individual along lines designed to further and more efficiently manifest and express the dominant desires of the individual. You have seen how Desire Power presses into service the powers of the subconscious mentality in the work of manifesting and expressing the strong desires. You have seen how the subconscious powers act so as to attract to the individual the things, person, conditions and circumstances serving to enable him to better manifest and express his sovereign desires; and how, in the same way, they tend to attract the individual to those things, persons, conditions and circumstances. You have seen how Desire Attraction works silently, even when one is asleep, toward the end impressed upon it by the character of the strong desires.

You have discovered the importance of "knowing exactly what you want," and have learned how to gain such important knowledge by Self-Analysis and Selection. You have discovered the importance of "wanting it hard enough," and have learned how to feed the Flame of Desire so as to cause it to burn fiercely. You have learned how to set into motion and activity the great body of Elemental Desire, and how to cause it to flow forth through the channels of manifestation and expression which you have carefully built for its flood. You have discovered the necessity of "paying the price of attainment" of the objects of your desire, and have learned the general rules concerning such payment.

You have been informed concerning the tremendous power of the Desire Power within your being, and have become acquainted with the laws governing its manifestation and expression, and the rules regulating its control and direction. If you have entered into the spirit of this instruction, and have allowed its influence to descend into the subconscious depths of your mentality, you have already become aware of the aroused energy of the Desire Power in those depths. You will have found yourself filled with a new and unfolding consciousness of Personal Power within you. You will have experienced that intuitive feeling that there have been set into operation in you certain subtle but dynamic forces which will tend to make you "stronger, better and more efficient."

As you proceed to arouse into further activity these great forces of your nature, and to direct their channel of manifestation and expression, you will from time to time receive actual evidence and proof that you are travelling along the right road, and are employing the proper methods. You will be astonished to receive proofs and actual results in the most unexpected manner, and from sources and directions never dreamt of before. You will realize more and more, as you proceed, that you have set into operation one of Nature's most potent forces, in fact, "the force of forces." Finally, you will begin to realize that the very actual presence within you of a Dominant Desire which has won its place in the "struggle for existence," and which has stood all the tests, is practically "the prophecy of its own fulfillment."

You have been asked to consider the facts which have been discovered concerning the nature, character and modes of activity of Desire Power, that great elemental psychic energy which is seen to pervade all existence and to be present universally. Analyze the actions of any or every living thing, and you will find Desire Power inspiring and motivating it. Nay, examine the motions of the so-called inanimate objects of Nature, and you will find even there the energizing forces of "something like Desire Power."

If Nature be regarded as a magnificent Cosmic Machine—then Desire Power is the motive-power that runs that universal machinery. If Nature be regarded as a Living Macrocosm—then Desire Power is the living motive-power inspiring and causing its activities. From whatever angle Nature may be viewed, under whatever hypothesis or theory it may be regarded, Desire Power is perceived to be the Something or Somewhat directly responsible for making "the wheels go 'round." The old Hermetic axiom, "As above, so below; as within, so without; as in great, so in small," is seen to apply here: the individual and the Cosmos both are seen to have as their essential motive-power that original, aboriginal, elemental, fundamental Something which we know as Desire Power.

In view of this fact, you scarcely need to be urged to study the methods of operation of this mighty force, so that you may harness it to your machinery of life and action. Like Gravitation or Electricity, its power is available to all who have the courage, intelligence and perseverance to master it and to press it into service. It is as free as the air or the sunshine; it costs nothing to run your living machinery with it—nothing but persistence and determination. You do not have to supply it with power, or to add energy to it: it has within itself far more power, energy or force than you will ever have occasion to make use of. All that you need do is to tap on to its free energy, and to set it to work for you in the direction of running the mental and physical machinery with which you have provided it.

Let us ask you to consider the following remarkable statement of Wr. Wilfrid Lay. Speaking of the Desire Power of the Subconscious, Dr. Lay says:

I call your attention to the enormous power of the Subconscious. It is the accumulated desire in each one of us, of aeons of evolution, the present form, in each individual, of that vital force which has kept itself immortal through thousands of generations of men behind us, and millions of generations of animals behind them. It need not be anything but a source of power to us, power that we can draw upon, if we rightly understand it, just as we can turn on power from a steam pipe or an electric wire. It need not be destructive, indeed it is not destructive, except in the most distracted souls, but on the contrary ought in each one of us, when we have learned to manage it rightly, to be as much and as completely at our command as is the power in the automobile. As in the automobile, there are a few simple things that we have to learn and the rest is furnished by the maker of the car, and we do ill to tamper with it. The experience of having a two-hundred-horsepower car placed at one's command (if it is to be driven by oneself) is a situation into which there are many persons, both men and women, who are very loath to enter. And similarly there are many persons who for various causes would not be willing to have developed the two-hundred-thousand-generation-power which resides in them. To all intents and purposes, and as far as human flesh is able to bear the strain, this power which is largely in the hands of the Subconscious in most men and women is illimitable.

Desire Power is a Cosmic Force designed for the controlled and directed use of the strong. It is at the disposal of all—but only few are courageous and determined enough to avail themselves of its services. The masses of men merely dally with it, play with it, handle it gingerly: the Masters of Men boldly grasp its controlling levers, and turn its power into their mental and physical machinery. It is a Master Force fitted only for the service of Masters. It is the rightful servant only of those whose slogan is: "I Can, I Will; I Dare, I Do!"

You can be a Master of Desire Power, and thus a Master of Men, a Master of Circumstances, a Master of Life, if you but will to be so. You are the Master of your Fate—the Captain of your Soul—if you will but recognize, realize and manifest the Power of the "I AM I" which is your Real Self, and of which Desire Power is the willing servant.

YOUR SILENT PARTNER WITHIN

While the mental planes lying outside of and beyond the field of ordinary consciousness have been until recent years comparatively unexplored by psychologists, and in fact have been almost entirely ignored by western psychology until modern times, the best thought of the present time is in practical agreement upon the fact that on those hidden planes of mentality are performed the major portion of our mental work, and that in their field are in operation some of the most important of our mental processes.

The exploration of these obscure regions of the mind has been one of the most fascinating tasks of modern psychology; and the mines have yielded rich material in abundance. Many mental phenomena formerly either denied as impossible by the orthodox psychologists, or else regarded by the average person as evidence of supernatural agencies and forces, are now seen to fit perfectly into the natural order of things, and to operate according to natural law and order. Not only have such investigations resulted in a greater increase of the scientific knowledge concerning the inner workings of the mind, but they have also served to place in the hands of the more advanced psychologists the material which they have turned to practical and efficient use by means of scientific methods of application.

The effect of these discoveries has been the presentation of an important truth to the thinking individual—the truth that his mental realm is a far greater and grander land that he has heretofore considered it to be. No longer is the Self held to be limited in its mental activities to the narrow field of ordinary consciousness. Your mental kingdom has suddenly expanded until it now constitutes a great empire, with borders flung wide and far beyond the boundaries of the little kingdom which you have been considering as the entire area of the field of the forces, powers and activities of the Self.

The Self has often been likened to the king of a great mental kingdom; but, in view of the discovery of the new facts concerning the wonderful field of the unconscious, subconscious and superconscious mental activities, the Self is now more properly to be represented as a mighty emperor of a vast empire of which only a comparatively small portion has as yet been explored. You are being called upon to appreciate more fully the ancient aphorism: "You are greater than you know." Your Self is like a new Columbus, gazing at the great new world which it has discovered around itself, and of which it is the owner and the ruler.

Employing the term, "The Subconscious," to indicate the entire field of activities of the mind which are performed below, above or in anyway "outside of" the field or plane of the ordinary consciousness of the individual, we soon discover that the activities of the Subconscious extend over a very wide range of manifestation, and embrace a great variety of forms of expression.

In the first place, the Subconscious presides over the activities of your physical organism; it is the animating spirit of your physical processes. It performs the manifold tasks of digestion, assimilation, nutrition, elimination, secretion, circulation, reproduction—in short, all of your vital processes. Your conscious mentality is thus relieved of these great tasks.

Again, the Subconscious supervises the performance of your instinctive actions. Every action that you perform automatically, instinctively, "by habit," "by heart" and without conscious employment of thought and will, is really performed by your subconscious mentality. Your conscious mentality, thus relieved of this work, is able to concentrate upon those other tasks which it alone can perform. When you learn to perform an action "by heart," or "by habit," the conscious mentality has turned over this particular work to your Subconscious.

Again, the Subconscious is largely concerned with the activities of your emotional nature. Your emotions which rise to the plane or level of consciousness are but the surface manifestations of the more elemental activities performed in the depths of the ocean of the Subconscious. Your elemental and instinctive emotions have their source and home in the Subconscious; they have accumulated there by reason of habit, heredity or racial memory. Practically all the material of your emotional activities is stored on the planes and levels of the Subconscious.

Again, the Subconscious presides over the processes of Memory. The subconscious planes or levels of the mind constitute the great storehouse of the recorded impressions of memory. Moreover, on those planes or levels is performed the work of indexing and cross-indexing the memory-records, by means of which subsequent recollection, recognition and remembrance are rendered possible. These regions of your subconscious mentality contain not only the recorded impressions of your own personal experience, but also those racial memories or inherited memories which manifest in you as "instinct," and which play a very important part in your life.

Again, the Subconscious is able to, and frequently does, perform for you important work along the lines of actual "thinking." By means of "mental rumination" it digests and assimilates the materials furnished by your conscious mentality, and then proceeds to classify these, to compare them, and to proceed to form judgments and decisions upon them and from them—all below the levels of your ordinary consciousness. Careful psychologists have decided that by far the greater part of our reasoning processes are really performed on mental levels and planes outside of the field of the ordinary consciousness. Much of your creative mental work, particularly that of the constructive imagination, is performed in this way, the result afterward being raised to the levels of conscious thought.

Finally, there are levels and planes "above" those of the ordinary consciousness, just as there are those "below" the latter. Just as the lower levels are largely concerned with working over the stored-up materials of the past, so these higher levels are concerned with reporting that which may be considered to represent the future conscious activities of the human race. These higher regions of the Subconscious may be said to contain the seed or embryo of the higher faculties and powers which will unfold fully in the future stages of the mental evolution of the race; many of these higher faculties and powers are even now beginning to manifest in occasional flashes in the minds of certain individuals, and, as a consequence, such individuals are frequently regarded as "inspired" or as possessing that indefinable quality or power known as "genius."

On these higher planes of the Subconscious abide certain marvelous powers of the Self, which powers manifest and express themselves in that which we call genius, inspiration, illumination—the exceptional mental achievements of certain intellects which stamp them as above the average. On these high planes abide and are manifested those wonderful mental activities which we attempt to explain under the term "Intuition." These activities, however, are not contrary to reason, though they may seem to transcend it at times; it is better to consider them as the manifestation of a Higher Reason. The investigation and exploration of these higher realms of the Subconscious form one of the most interesting and fascinating tasks of modern psychology. Even now, the reports of the investigators and explorers are of surpassing interest; those which confidently may be looked for in the future bid fair to constitute a marvelous contribution to the pages of the history of modern scientific research.

We shall ask you to accompany us in an exploration of the various regions of the Subconscious—those wonderful realms of your mind—from the highest to the lowest. In this new land there are valuable deposits of material useful to you and to all mankind. It is our purpose to point out these to you, and to instruct you in the most approved methods of mining and converting them to practical uses. You are interested in the matter of being led directly to the mines containing these rich deposits, and in being told just how to conduct the mining operations and the converting processes. In this spirit, then, our journey of exploration shall be conducted.

The Secret Forces of the Great Subconscious, like all other great natural forces, may be harnessed and pressed into service by you. Like electricity, they may be so managed and directed into the proper channels that they may be set to work by and for you. You have been employing these forces, to a greater or less extent, in very many of your mental activities; but, in all probability, you have been employing them instinctively and without a full knowledge of the laws and principles involved in them. When you understand just what these forces are, how they work, and the methods best calculated to produce efficient results and effects, then you may proceed to employ them intelligently, deliberately and with conscious purpose and intent, end and aim.

The average man employs but about 25 per cent of the Subconscious Power. The man who understands the principles and methods to which we have just referred will be able to employ 100 per cent of his available Subconscious Power. This means that he will be able to increase fourfold his Subconscious mental work and activity, with correspondingly increased results and effects. Inasmuch as at least 75 per cent of man's mental processes are performed on the plane or level of the Subconscious, it will be seen that the benefits arising from quadrupling his Subconscious mental activities and available power are almost beyond the power of adequate calculation. This increased power and efficiency, moreover, are not obtained at the cost of increased effort and mental wear and tear: on the contrary, the man effectively employing his Subconscious relieves himself of a great portion of the mental strain incident to the employment of the conscious mentality.

In addition to the offices and powers of the Super-conscious which we have mentioned, there is another and a most important function of that phase of the mentality which may be called "the protective power." Many persons, most persons in fact, have at times experienced this beneficent power. They have felt strongly that they were in close contact with a force, power or entity of some kind which was in some way higher than themselves, but which was concerned with their welfare. This beneficent presence has been interpreted in various ways in accordance with the trend of thought of those experiencing it. Some of the ancients called it "the kindly genius"; others termed it "the guardian angel"; still others have thought of it as "my spirit friend"; while many others, though quite vividly conscious of its presence and power, have failed to give it a special name.

But by whatever name it may have been thought of, or even when no name at all has been applied to it, the mysterious something has been recognized as a beneficent presence-power—a hovering and brooding Something or Somewhat animated by a warm, kindly interest in the individual, and seemingly devoted to his interests and disposed to render to him useful services.

This beneficent presence-power has often acted as a warning guardian in the lives of many persons. In other cases it has been felt to have acted subtly to bring about advantageous results and conditions for the persons whom it protected. It has led some into circumstances and conditions calculated to be of advantage to them; it has drawn others away from conditions and circumstances calculated to bring harm to them. In short, it has played the part of "the kindly genius" or "the guardian angel" to many an individual.

The touch of this Unseen Hand has been felt by countless individuals—very likely by you who are now reading these lines. It has cheered men when the tide of circumstances seemed to be running against them; it has animated them with a new lively spirit, has encouraged them to renewed endeavor, has filled them with new courage when they needed it most. It has seemingly led persons into the presence of other persons and things, into conditions and environments, which have proved advantageous to them. Men in all ages—some of the most practical and "hard headed" men of affairs, among others—have felt the touch of this Unseen Hand, and have gratefully acknowledged its help in times of need, even though they have been perplexed concerning its real character.

To many careful thinkers who have earnestly investigated this phenomenon, it has seemed that this beneficent presence-power—this Unseen Hand that has reached out in times of need—is not an external power, nor an entity outside of themselves, but is rather a manifestation of that part of man's mental nature which we have here considered under the term "The Superconscious." Instead of being an entity outside of us, it is believed to be a part of ourselves— a phase, part or aspect of our Self that manifests above the levels or planes of the ordinary consciousness. In short, this "kindly genius" or "guardian angel" is your own Superconscious Self, manifesting on some of its higher levels or planes of activity and power.

In this Higher Self you have a friend far truer, more constant and more loyal than can be any other friend—for it is Yourself, in its essence and substance. Your interests are its interests, for you are one with it in essential being and power. It will manifest a fidelity to you, and a watchfulness over your real interests which is amazing in its devotion and constancy. It will manifest toward you, in turns, the protecting care of a father; the brooding watchful, loving care of a mother; and the helpful, fraternal care of a brother. It will be all of these things to you—and more—if you will but give it the chance to unfold its presence and to manifest its power in your life.

This Higher Self—this phase of your Superconscious—needs but the encouragement of your recognition and realization in order to manifest its power in your behalf. It is seemingly discouraged, disheartened and abashed by your indifference, unbelief and the failure to recognize its presence and to realize its power. It does not need "training" or "developing"—all that it asks is to be recognized and realized by you, and to have from you a kindly, sympathetic reception. It has done much for you in the past—it will do more for you in the future, if you will but meet it half way.

This higher part of your Self is full of discernment, and of cold, keen-edged wisdom. It can see far ahead, and is able to discern and select the right road for you to travel, and then to lead you into that road and to keep your feet on its solid substance, in spite of your efforts to take a side path or to wander into the ditches which lie on either side of the road. You will do well to "get off by yourself" once in a while, then and there to commune with your Higher Self—to have a little "heart-to-heart" visit with it. You will find this Higher Self to be a wonderful companion—one closer to you than can be any human being—for it is Yourself, and nothing but Yourself, manifesting on the higher planes and levels of your being. You will emerge from these periods of self-communion with renewed strength and vigor, filled with new hope and faith, animated by new ambitions and purposive determination.

The Magic Word

We have presented to you a view of your New Mental Empire—a view of its lowest and its highest planes and levels, of its highlands and its lowlands. It is your own empire—YOURS! Yours it is to rule and to govern, to explore and to cultivate. You are at home in it. The many wonderful phenomena manifested in its immense region are your phenomena—yours to control, direct, develop, cultivate; yours to restrict, restrain, inhibit; at your will, as you will, by your will.

Do not allow yourself to be tempted by the wonderful powers manifested by some of your subordinate mental machinery or instruments; do not allow yourself to fall under the spell of any of the phenomenal manifestations in your mental wonderland. View all; respect all; use all; demand and secure aid and work from all; but never lose sight of the fact that YOU, your Real Self—the "I am I"—is the Master of this land, the ruler of this Empire, and that you rightfully have power and dominion over it, all its inhabitants, and all contained in its realm.

Your "I am I," your Real Self—YOU—are a centre of consciousness and will, of Personal Power, in that Infinite and Eternal Power, that Ultimate POWER from which all things proceed, and in which we live, and move, and have our being. Your physical body and your physical energies; your mental mechanism and its energies, manifesting on any or all the planes or levels of consciousness, subconsciousness, or superconsciousness; all these are but instruments or channels of expression of your Real Self, the "I AM I," of YOU.

YOU, the "I AM I" are the centre of your personal world of experience and manifestation. Keep ever your rightful place at the center of that world; observe all the rest whirling and revolving around that center, as the planets revolve, whirling, around the sun. YOU are the Sun! Do not lose your balance, nor be induced to move away from your central position to accommodate any of your subordinate planets—not even the greatest of them.

Hail! Mighty Emperor! Enter into and possess, rule and govern, your New Mental Empire! It is YOURS!

Let us remind you of the truth of the ancient aphorism:

"You are greater than you know!"